Holly is a local celebrity chef—
happy cooking!

Christmas 2006

Holly Clegg's Trim & Terrific™

Home Entertaining the Easy Way

Holly Clegg's Trim & Terrific™

Home Entertaining the Easy Way

FAST AND DELICIOUS RECIPES FOR EVERY OCCASION

by Holly Berkowitz Clegg

Photography by David Humphreys

COURAGE
BOOKS

AN IMPRINT OF RUNNING PRESS
PHILADELPHIA • LONDON

9   8   7   6   5   4   3   2   1
Digit on the right indicates the number of this printing

Library of Congress Control Number: 2002115225

ISBN 0-7624-1629-7

Food styling by Danielle Chapman
Creative consulting by Pamela Clegg Hill
In-house editing by Katie Greczylo
Cover design by Bill Jones
Interior design by Rosemary Tottoroto
Typography: Officina Sans and Officina Serif

This book may be ordered by mail from the publisher.
But try your bookstore first!

Published by Courage Books, an imprint of
Running Press Book Publishers
125 South Twenty-second Street
Philadelphia, Pennsylvania 19103-4399

Visit us on the web!
www.runningpress.com

DISHES/PARTIES PICTURED ON COVER:
Front cover: Holiday Dinner (page 84)
Back cover (clockwise): Barbecue Shrimp (page 109), The Big Enchilada (page 42),
Tiramisu (page 78), and Bountiful Brunch (page 14)

Also by Holly Clegg*

The Holly Clegg Trim & Terrific™ Cookbook

Meals on the Move: Rush Hour Recipes

Eating Well Through Cancer: Easy Recipes & Recommendations During and After Treatment

*To order these books by Holly Clegg, call 1-800-88HOLLY or visit her website at www.hollyclegg.com.

Table of Contents

Acknowledgments

I owe my family an abundance of thanks for their patience and unconditional support. To my husband Mike, who tolerated hours of cooking and a house in a whirlwind while we photographed each party. You listened attentively to all of my stories and even my complaints with lots of love and encouragement. To Haley, my tenth grader, who allowed me to miss soccer games and found many alternative rides home but always had a smile on her face and a big hug for me every night. To Courtney, my sophomore at George Washington University, who tested recipes over the holidays and viewed via email all the party pictures so I could share every moment with my cooking soul mate. To Todd, my son, now working in New York in investment banking, who knows how much I treasure our phone chats. You insist that there always be a ridiculous amount of food in this house when you're home, but you manage to eat it all! To Robert, my stepson, who was always willing to grill, taste, or give a helping hand whenever needed. And to my loyal dachshunds, Flappy and Elvis, who followed me everywhere, whether I was cooking in the kitchen (where the occasional scrap might fall) or typing recipes in my office. Thanks for the companionship!

To Mae Mae, who does it all from babysitting to setting up props and fine-tuning details—a very special thanks for picking berries from my yard to fill the vase for my holiday party! I couldn't do it without you, mother Mae Mae! To Pam, my Clegg sis, who flew in from Denver to help cook in preparation for the photo shoots—and thank goodness, because neither of us ever imagined the tremendous volume of work this required. You are my right hand, but most importantly, thanks for running to the grocery store every morning! I enjoyed toasting to the end of each day with you. My thanks to Jim for sharing the Western public relations socialite. To Nana and Papa, who taught me this about entertaining a long time ago: use everything you have and don't worry if it breaks! And thanks to Aunt Garney, the true party Goux girl. To Ilene, my sister, confidante, best friend, and recipient of daily phone calls—what would I do without you? The "Short Cuts" sections are dedicated to you, as I know this will be where you'll turn. Thanks also to Bart, my party animal brother-in-law who's always ready to have a good time—when he is not doctoring. Michael and Kim, true wine connoisseurs, if I could only remember what you said! And where my love of cooking began so many years ago (who's counting?), thank you to my parents, Ruth and Jerry in Fort Worth, who encouraged me to pursue my dreams. You instilled in me the belief that if I worked hard, I could accomplish my goals, thereby giving me the best gift a daughter could ask for—a belief in myself. I wish you were in town to enjoy the food!

To my friends, who I have entertained at my home for years. Thanks to Francine, always #1, who is there for me whenever I surface, and to Doll, the fish supplier. Louann, thanks for your helping hand with everything from cooking to kids, and Ronnie, you are the true king of blackened redfish and my #1 doctor. Thanks to Gail, my long time friend, and Lewis, Mary, my dear friend, and Rob, Lynell (my groupie), and Jeff. To Gerald, the fabulous coauthor of my cancer cookbook, and his wife, Melinda; Bev, my entertaining buddy, and Johnny; Karen, my talking-exercise friend, and Anthony, who better keep me looking good; Melanie, my artist buddy, and Tommy; Louise and Jim; and Anisa and Trent. To the Cliffords, the Sligars, and the Mocklers, we have shared lots of fun times and memories. To Jim and Luella, for both business and fun for so many years. To my college buddies around the country, Lila, Leslie, Sherri, Jolie, Jo, and Missy, who graciously entertain or dine with me whenever I pop in town. And to my Fort Worth cooking inspirations, who always shared recipes and entertaining ideas with me from my very first memories of loving food—thanks, Marcia, #1 cook of all time, Selma, with your flair for entertaining, and Joyce, #1 taster.

To Al, my creative counselor, and Diane, Nancy, Danielle, and Moria of Diane Allen & Associates, thanks for a working friendship relationship that I treasure. Thanks to the Louisiana Sweet Potato Commission for making me their Sweet Potato Queen! Robin, Mary, and Rosemary at Dublin & Associates, you know how I value working with you and our times together. Kate at Campbell's Soup, Inc., I am not letting you out of my web.

And thanks to those directly involved with this wonderful book. Kendall for keeping me organized. Tammi Hancock of Hancock Nutrition, thanks for another terrific job with the analysis and letting me party a little extra. Steve Labens, from Cut Flower in Baton Rouge, thanks for your expertise in the incredible flowers. Danielle, your talent is evident in your styling throughout the gorgeous pictures. And thanks is not a big enough word to express my gratitude for the outstanding job done by photographer David Humphreys. I had a vision and I still get excited looking and each and every picture. Excellence at its best!

To those at Running Press who make this possible. What would I do if I didn't have you, Carlo DeVito? You are the reason I am a Running Press girl in the first place, so you'll have to listen to all my phone calls forever, sorry. To Jennifer Brunn for her patience in dealing with me as I talk and go in every direction. Thanks for organizing all my travels and beyond, which I know is a full time job. Bill Jones, from our first meeting I knew your enthusiasm would make this the most beautiful and functional book ever! To Katie Greczylo, my talented in-house editor who has a flair with my words, answers every one of my questions (and there are a lot) efficiently—thanks for coordinating this huge undertaking. To Justin Schwartz, thanks for the outside editing. To John Whalen, I appreciate all your effort and excitement for my books—I know that without you, I would be in big trouble. To Sarah Wolf, keep those incredible sales going! And last but not least, thank you Buz Teacher for believing in me once again.

And a thank you to all my media buddies throughout the United States from print to television, some of whom I have been nagging for years. Thanks for including me.

Finally, the biggest thanks must go again to all my Trim & Terrific™ supporters who have supported me for many years. Thank you for giving me the opportunity to share my recipes and party ideas in your home. Now, you know the rules, *get to cooking!*

Introduction

Even though a standard dictionary defines the word *entertain* as "to keep pleasantly interested" or "to extend hospitality towards," many potential hosts and hostesses often have an *unpleasant* reaction to the word. When entertaining is mentioned, my sister immediately feels intimidated, and my mother stresses as she begins creating numerous lists. I personally enjoy entertaining at home, whether I'm hosting a casual, last-minute gathering or an elegant cocktail party. My sister-in-law also loves to throw a good party, and whenever she has one in the works, she calls me enthusiastically for recipe suggestions. Everyone approaches entertaining and party planning in their own way, but whether you look forward to having company or feel pressured just thinking about it, you can always use an easy, practical source of menu suggestions and decorating ideas.

I have read numerous party and entertaining books, and many of them make even me, the enthusiastic and experienced hostess, feel anxious. You need to hire a party planner just to help you interpret those books and a staff to prepare all the recipes, not to mention have an unlimited budget. But what do you do when you need fast, easy recipes and tips for throwing a fun, affordable, at-home fiesta? *Holly Clegg's Trim & Terrific™ Home Entertaining the Easy Way* is here to make a difference in your life!

I have specifically designed this book to make entertaining easy and enjoyable. Whether you are inviting friends over to watch the big game, having family members join you for Sunday dinner, or throwing a complete extravaganza, this book will give you the guidance you need to entertain with ease in the comfort of your own home. And there are no set rules to follow, so you can feel free to select your favorite recipes, take short cuts as needed, and add your own personal touch. I only insist that you keep things easy on yourself, so you will actually enjoy the event!

I have included a variety of recipes from which to select when planning your chosen party. The menu at the beginning of each chapter is only a guide—while I've shared some of my favorite recipe combinations here, I've also included dishes that are perfect for several different types of parties, so don't hesitate to mix and match. After all, it's your party! Try serving the Chocolate Espresso Brownies (see page 59) in the Terrific Tailgating chapter for your dessert party, or use the Spinach Artichoke Dip (see page 64) from the Backyard Barbecue at your cocktail party. But don't limit these recipes to parties only—keep in mind that they are also perfect for everyday cooking.

People are often overwhelmed at the thought of all they need accomplish before the guests arrive. For every menu, I have provided handy "Short Cuts," quick and easy options for reducing the amount of preparation while still allowing you to add your personal touch on the party. For a truly successful soiree, take on only those tasks with which you are comfortable, and then supplement with food and decorations from other sources (supermarket, bakery, deli, or florist) as needed. As for those of you who want to throw a party with unique flair, the "Exciting Extras" give you additional ideas. Flowers, paper goods, and even extra food serving suggestions will help you boost your creativity. Check out the "Terrific Tips" sprinkled throughout the book for even more great ideas and explanations.

I've been writing cookbooks for years, and my readers have often requested that I include photography in my books. I am thrilled to now offer you a wonderful array of full-color photos to accompany my equally colorful recipes and entertaining tidbits. Each specific party was photographed in my home, giving you a glimpse of my personal style of entertaining.

As in my other books, most of the recipes require less than 30 minutes to prepare, and they are made with familiar ingredients you most likely already have in your home. I have also included nutritional analyses and diabetic exchanges with each recipe, so you can entertain the true Trim & Terrific™ way. In my last book, the Freezer-Friendly and Vegetarian icons were so popular that I have included them once again. And most exciting, this entertaining book is packed with all *new* recipes to help you throw a fun, fabulous, and delicious party. *Holly Clegg's Trim & Terrific™ Home Entertaining the Easy Way* will inspire you to entertain friends and family in the comfort of your home, and you will be ready to celebrate every occasion!

Holly Clegg

A GUIDE TO SYMBOLS

 Vegetarian recipe

 Freezer-Friendly recipe

NOTE: When there is a range for the yield, the nutritional analysis is always calculated on the larger number of servings.

Bountiful Brunch

For many of us, weekday mornings are rushed, if not chaotic, and breakfast is often eaten on the go. But on the weekends or special occasions, we can trade in the cereal bars and hasty cups of joe for a leisurely brunch to be enjoyed with family and friends.

Instead of traditional dishes of scrambled eggs, sausage, and toast, I prefer to offer a menu packed with exciting flavors and twists while still using familiar ingredients. Those of you with a sweet tooth will especially enjoy the fabulous Baked Praline French Toast. If you prefer eggs, the Mediterranean Breakfast Bake is the perfect choice. And for an exceptional and savory selection, try the Shrimp and Cheese Grits Casserole. Quick breads and sweet rolls created from store-bought biscuits make baking at home nearly effortless, and a serving of rich Mocha Coffee Punch will save you a trip to your favorite coffee shop. Select the dishes that tempt your palate, and mix-and-match to create your own menu. All my brunch recipes are convenient make-ahead dishes, allowing you to sit down and delight in your company. I recommend serving your brunch buffet-style for a more casual atmosphere.

Brunches can be intimate, but they certainly lend themselves to larger gatherings. When my daughter was home from college for the holidays, I served brunch for fifteen of her friends. Whether you are celebrating the holiday season or enjoying the freshness of spring, these simple recipes will tantalize your taste buds in a nutritious and deliciously memorable morning-to-afternoon meal.

MENU SELECTIONS

EXCITING EXTRAS

▶ Create delightful table decorations by using inexpensive small clay pots to display seasonal flowers.

▶ Place your favorite flowers in small bud vases and arrange them casually among the dishes on your table.

▶ Wrap forks in cloth or paper napkins and tie with ribbon ahead of time. One of the conveniences of a brunch menu is that a fork is often the only utensil your guests will need!

▶ Garnish smoothies with fresh strawberries for an added touch of color and flavor.

▶ Serve smoothies in small glasses on a tray or platter as a starter.

Short Cuts

▶ Serve smoothies
purchased from your local
smoothie shop instead
of making them yourself.
▶ Pick up fresh muffins or
bread at a local bakery.
▶ Order a fruit tray from
your supermarket and
transfer to a bowl.

Baked Praline French Toast with Orange Sauce

If I had to stand and cook each piece of French toast individually, I would never serve it for guests! For greater ease, I came up with this amazing, overnight, one-dish recipe. The brown sugar caramelizes to form a delicious praline sauce on the bottom of the dish. To add even more flavor, I serve the toast with the Orange Sauce or warm maple syrup—either way, it's a winner.

MAKES 12 SERVINGS

6 tablespoons (3/4 stick) margarine
1 cup light brown sugar
2 tablespoons light corn syrup
1/2 cup chopped pecans (optional)
2 eggs
3 egg whites
1 cup orange juice
1/4 cup sugar
1/3 cup skim milk
1 teaspoon grated orange rind
1 teaspoon vanilla extract
1/2 teaspoon ground cinnamon
1 (16-ounce) loaf French bread,
 cut into 12 to 15 (1-inch) slices
2/3 cup Orange Sauce (recipe follows),
 for serving

In a microwaveable dish, combine the margarine, brown sugar, and corn syrup. Microwave until the margarine has melted and the brown sugar has dissolved, about 1 minute. Pour the mixture into an ungreased, 3-quart oblong baking dish. Sprinkle with pecans, if desired.

In a large bowl, whisk together the eggs, egg whites, orange juice, sugar, skim milk, orange rind, vanilla, and cinnamon.

Arrange the bread slices over the brown sugar mixture in the baking dish. Pour the egg mixture over the bread slices. Cover with plastic wrap and refrigerate for at least 1 hour or overnight.

Prior to serving, preheat the oven to 350°F.

Bake for about 30 minutes. Serve immediately, each piece topped with some of the praline sauce that forms on bottom of the baking dish. For additional flavor, top with the Orange Sauce or maple syrup.

Nutritional Information per Serving (without Orange Sauce)
Calories 288, Protein (g) 6, Carbohydrate (g) 49, Fat (g) 8, Calories from Fat (%) 24, Saturated Fat (g) 1, Dietary Fiber (g) 2, Cholesterol (mg) 36, Sodium (mg) 336
Diabetic Exchanges: *1.5 starch, 1.5 other carbohydrate, 1 fat*

Orange Sauce

*Tangy and sweet, this sauce compliments Baked Praline French Toast perfectly.
I present it in a separate dish so that each person can pour some over his or her own serving, if desired.
This sauce also tastes great when poured over plain cake or ice cream—the low-fat variety, of course!*

MAKES 2/3 CUP, OR 12 SERVINGS

1/4 cup (1/2 stick) margarine
1/4 cup sugar
1/4 cup orange juice
2 tablespoons orange liqueur (optional)

In a small saucepan over low heat, combine the margarine, sugar, and orange juice, and cook, stirring occasionally, until the mixture comes to a boil. Remove from the heat, and whisk until the mixture is slightly thickened. Stir in the orange liqueur, if desired. Serve warm.

Nutritional Information per Serving
Calories 52, Protein (g) 0, Carbohydrate (g) 5, Fat (g) 4, Calories from Fat (%) 64, Saturated Fat (g) 1, Dietary Fiber (g) 0, Cholesterol (mg) 0, Sodium (mg) 44
Diabetic Exchanges: *0.5 other carbohydrate, 1 fat*

Terrific Tip
DON'T THROW AWAY THAT STALE BREAD! THE CONCEPT OF DIPPING BREAD INTO A MILK AND EGG MIXTURE, THEN FRYING IT UNTIL GOLDEN BROWN ON BOTH SIDES, DID INDEED ORIGINATE IN FRANCE. IT WAS DEVELOPED AS A WAY OF REVIVING FRENCH BREAD, WHICH BECOMES DRY AFTER ONLY A DAY OR TWO.

Mediterranean Breakfast Bake

A spectrum of seasonings and vegetables with a touch of feta cheese turns a traditional breakfast item into an extraordinary dish.

MAKES 10 TO 12 SERVINGS

1 (16-ounce) loaf day-old French bread,
  cut into 1-inch slices

5 eggs

4 egg whites

3 cups skim milk

2 tablespoons Dijon mustard

1 teaspoon dried oregano leaves

Salt and pepper, to taste

1/2 pound fresh mushrooms, sliced

1 onion, chopped

1 teaspoon minced garlic

1 (10-ounce) package fresh baby spinach

1 tablespoon all-purpose flour

6 small tomatoes, thinly sliced

2 ounces feta cheese, crumbled

1 1/2 cups shredded part-skim mozzarella
  cheese, divided

Coat a 13 x 9 x 2-inch baking dish with nonstick cooking spray. Place half of the bread slices in the bottom of the baking dish.

In a mixing bowl, beat the eggs, egg whites, milk, mustard, oregano, salt, and pepper. Set aside.

Coat a large skillet with nonstick cooking spray, and set over medium heat. Add the mushrooms, onion, and garlic, and cook, stirring, until the vegetables are tender, about 5 minutes. Add the spinach and flour, and cook, stirring, until spinach is wilted, 2 to 3 minutes. Season with salt and pepper.

Spread the mushroom-spinach mixture over the bread slices in the baking dish. Top with the sliced tomatoes and feta cheese. Sprinkle 1 cup of the shredded mozzarella cheese over the top. Top with the remaining bread slices. Sprinkle with remaining 1/2 cup of mozzarella cheese. Pour the egg mixture over the casserole, and refrigerate for at least 2 hours or overnight.

Prior to serving, preheat the oven to 350°F. Bake for 40 to 50 minutes, or until puffed and golden. Serve immediately.

Nutritional Information per Serving
Calories 238, Protein (g) 15, Carbohydrate (g) 29, Fat (g) 7, Calories from Fat (%) 26, Saturated Fat (g) 3, Dietary Fiber (g) 3, Cholesterol (mg) 102, Sodium (mg) 512
Diabetic Exchanges: *1.5 lean meat, 1.5 starch, 1 vegetable*

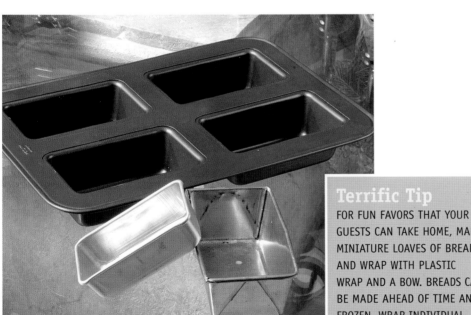

Terrific Tip
FOR FUN FAVORS THAT YOUR GUESTS CAN TAKE HOME, MAKE MINIATURE LOAVES OF BREAD AND WRAP WITH PLASTIC WRAP AND A BOW. BREADS CAN BE MADE AHEAD OF TIME AND FROZEN. WRAP INDIVIDUAL LOAVES IN PLASTIC WRAP AND PUT IN ZIPPER-TOP PLASTIC BAGS BEFORE PLACING THEM IN THE FREEZER.

Shrimp and Cheese Grits Casserole

Shrimp and grits pair together wonderfully in this incredible, make-ahead casserole. Be sure to use the quick grits, not instant.

MAKES 10 TO 12 SERVINGS

1½ cups quick grits

6 cups water

2 cups shredded reduced-fat
 sharp Cheddar cheese, divided
 (use white Cheddar, if available)

¾ cup freshly grated Parmesan cheese

1 teaspoon paprika

⅛ teaspoon cayenne pepper

3 ounces chopped lean ham

Salt and pepper, to taste

2 pounds medium-size shrimp, peeled

1½ pounds sliced fresh mushrooms

3 teaspoons minced garlic

¼ cup dry white wine (optional)

3 tablespoons lemon juice

1½ cups sliced green onions (scallions)

Cook the grits in the water according to the instructions on the package. When the grits are ready, stir in 1½ cups of the Cheddar cheese, the Parmesan cheese, paprika, and cayenne until the cheese is melted. Stir in the ham, and set aside.

Coat a large skillet with nonstick cooking spray and set over medium-high heat. Add the shrimp, mushrooms, and garlic, and cook, stirring, until the shrimp are fully pink and almost done, 3 to 5 minutes. Add the wine, if desired, and the lemon juice, and cook, stirring, until the shrimp are done, about a minute longer. Remove from the heat.

In a large bowl, mix together the grits mixture and the shrimp mixture, and season with salt and pepper. Stir in the green onions. Coat a 2-quart casserole dish with nonstick cooking spray. Transfer the grits and shrimp mixture to the prepared dish.

Sprinkle the dish with the remaining ½ cup of Cheddar cheese, and serve immediately. If you are preparing this dish ahead of time, cover tightly with plastic wrap and refrigerate to store for up to 1 day, then bring to room temperature, and bake at 350°F for 20 to 30 minutes, or until heated through.

Nutritional Information per Serving
Calories 249, Protein (g) 26, Carbohydrate (g) 20, Fat (g) 6, Calories from Fat (%) 22, Saturated Fat (g) 3, Dietary Fiber (g) 2, Cholesterol (mg) 129, Sodium (mg) 389
Diabetic Exchanges: *3 lean meat, 1 starch, 1 vegetable*

Baked Spinach Soufflé

For vegetable lovers, this is a wonderfully light yet satisfying dish that makes a perfect addition to any brunch menu.

MAKES 8 TO 10 SERVINGS

2 (10-ounce) packages frozen chopped spinach
1 onion, chopped
1 teaspoon minced garlic
1 cup nonfat plain yogurt
1/2 cup fat-free sour cream
1 cup shredded reduced-fat sharp Cheddar cheese
2 eggs
2 egg whites
1 teaspoon Worcestershire sauce
1/4 teaspoon ground nutmeg
Salt and pepper, to taste

Preheat the oven to 350°F. Coat a 13 x 9 x 2-inch baking dish with nonstick cooking spray.

Prepare the frozen spinach according to the package directions, drain well, and set aside.

Coat a skillet with nonstick cooking spray, and set over medium heat. Add the onion and garlic, and cook, stirring, until tender, about 5 minutes. Remove from the heat.

In a large bowl, mix together the cooked spinach, the onion and garlic mixture, the yogurt, sour cream, Cheddar cheese, eggs, egg whites, Worcestershire sauce, nutmeg, salt, and pepper. Transfer the mixture to the prepared baking dish. Bake for about 40 minutes, or until the mixture is set. Serve immediately.

Nutritional Information per Serving
Calories 99, Protein (g) 9, Carbohydrate (g) 8, Fat (g) 3, Calories from Fat (%) 29, Saturated Fat (g) 2, Dietary Fiber (g) 2, Cholesterol (mg) 51, Sodium (mg) 172
Diabetic Exchanges: *1 lean meat, 0.5 starch*

Terrific Tip

NEVER PUT A REFRIGERATED GLASS BAKING DISH DIRECTLY INTO A HOT OVEN, AS THIS CAN CAUSE THE GLASS TO CRACK. BRING THE DISH TO ROOM TEMPER- ATURE FIRST OR PLACE THE COLD DISH IN A COLD OVEN AND LET IT HEAT UP WHILE THE OVEN PRE- HEATS, IN WHICH CASE YOU'LL HAVE TO LET THE RECIPE COOK A LITTLE LONGER THAN DIRECTED.

Terrific Tip

TO PREPARE THE BAKED SPINACH SOUFFLÉ IN ADVANCE, TIGHTLY COVER THE UNBAKED CASSE- ROLE WITH PLASTIC WRAP AND STORE IN THE REFRIGERATOR FOR UP TO 1 DAY. THEN BRING TO ROOM TEMPERATURE BEFORE BAKING AS DIRECTED.

Bowl of Berries

I am partial to fresh berries when they are available. However, other fruits may be added.

MAKES 8 SERVINGS

1 pound strawberries, stems removed and sliced
1 pound blueberries
1/2 cup confectioners' sugar
1 orange, squeezed
1/2 lemon, squeezed

In a serving bowl, toss together the strawberries and blueberries. In another small bowl, mix together the confectioners' sugar, orange juice, and lemon juice, stirring until the sugar dis- solves. Pour over the fruit, and gently toss to combine.

Nutritional Information per Serving
Calories 83, Protein (g) 1, Carbohydrate (g) 21, Fat (g) 0, Calories from Fat (%) 0, Saturated Fat (g) 0, Dietary Fiber (g) 3, Cholesterol (mg) 0, Sodium (mg) 4
Diabetic Exchanges: *1 fruit, 0.5 other carbohydrate*

Blintz Casserole with Strawberry Sauce

Rich, sweet, and satisfying describes this very popular recipe.
I love serving it with the Strawberry Sauce or a dollop of fat-free sour cream and fresh berries.

CHEESE FILLING:

1 (8-ounce) package reduced-fat cream cheese, softened

1 cup fat-free cottage cheese

1 egg

3 tablespoons sugar

1 tablespoon vanilla extract

1 teaspoon grated orange rind

BATTER:

¼ cup (½ stick) margarine, softened

⅓ cup sugar

2 eggs

2 egg whites

½ cup orange juice

1 cup all-purpose flour

2 teaspoons baking powder

1 cup fat-free sour cream

1½ cups Strawberry Sauce (recipe follows), for serving

Preheat the oven to 350°F. Coat a 2-quart oblong baking dish with nonstick cooking spray.

Prepare the Cheese Filling: In a mixing bowl, beat together the cream cheese, cottage cheese, egg, sugar, vanilla, and orange rind until smooth and creamy. Set aside.

Prepare the Batter: In a mixing bowl, beat together the margarine and sugar until creamy. Add the eggs, one at a time, and then the egg whites, beating well after each addition. Stir in the orange juice.

In a small bowl, mix together the flour and baking powder. Slowly add the flour mixture to the margarine mixture alternately with the sour cream, mixing just to combine after each addition and ending with flour mixture.

Pour half of the batter into the prepared baking dish. Top with the Cheese Filling. Spread the remaining batter on top, being careful not to mix it with the Cheese Filling. Bake for 45 minutes, or until golden brown and set. Serve with the Strawberry Sauce.

Nutritional Information per Serving (without Strawberry Sauce)
Calories 218, Protein (g) 9, Carbohydrate (g) 24, Fat (g) 9, Calories from Fat (%) 38, Saturated Fat (g) 4, Dietary Fiber (g) 0, Cholesterol (mg) 71, Sodium (mg) 311
Diabetic Exchanges: *1 lean meat, 1.5 other carbohydrate, 1 fat*

Strawberry Sauce

This homemade berry sauce is simple but adds that finishing touch of elegance.

2 (10-ounce) packages frozen strawberries in syrup, thawed

¼ cup sugar

2 tablespoons orange juice

Drain one of the packages of strawberries, and discard the juice. Place the fruit from both packages, including the juice from the second (undrained) package, the sugar, and orange juice in a food processor or blender, and process until smooth. Refrigerate, tightly covered, until ready to use.

Nutritional Information per Serving
Calories 59, Protein (g) 0, Carbohydrate (g)15, Fat (g) 0, Calories from Fat (%) 0, Saturated Fat (g) 0, Dietary Fiber (g) 0, Cholesterol (mg) 0, Sodium (mg) 2
Diabetic Exchanges: *1 other carbohydrate*

Terrific Tip

FOR A QUICK-AND-EASY SUBSTITUTE FOR THE STRAWBERRY SAUCE, HEAT UP A BERRY "REAL FRUIT" JAM, AND POUR SOME OVER EACH PORTION.

COCONUT BANANA BREAD

Coconut Banana Bread

Coconut and a lime glaze turn the ever-popular banana bread into a fabulous, rich-tasting quick bread.

MAKES 16 SERVINGS

3 tablespoons margarine, divided
and softened
2 tablespoons reduced-fat cream cheese
1 cup sugar
1 egg
2 cups all-purpose flour
2 teaspoons baking powder
1/2 teaspoon baking soda
1 cup mashed bananas
1/2 cup buttermilk
1 teaspoon coconut extract
1/3 cup flaked coconut
1/4 cup light brown sugar
1/4 tablespoon lime juice

Preheat the oven to 350°F. Coat a 9 x 5 x 3-inch loaf pan with nonstick cooking spray.

In a large mixing bowl, beat 2 tablespoons of the margarine and the cream cheese until creamy. Add the sugar, beating well. Add the egg, beating well. In a separate bowl, mix together the flour, baking powder, and baking soda, and set aside. In a small bowl, combine the mashed bananas and buttermilk, and set aside.

Slowly add the flour mixture to the cream cheese mixture alternately with the banana mixture, mixing just until combined after each addition, beginning and ending with portions of the flour mixture. Stir in the coconut. Pour the batter into the prepared pan. Bake for 50 to 60 minutes, or until an inserted toothpick comes out clean.

In a microwave-safe dish, mix together the brown sugar, the remaining 1 tablespoon of margarine, and the lime juice, and microwave for 45 seconds to 1 minute, or until bubbly. Pour over the hot bread. Cool the bread to room temperature before serving.

Nutritional Information per Serving
*Calories 171, Protein (g) 3, Carbohydrate (g) 33, Fat (g) 4, Calories from Fat (%) 19,
Saturated Fat (g) 1, Dietary Fiber (g) 1, Cholesterol (mg) 15, Sodium (mg) 151*
Diabetic Exchanges: *1 starch, 1 other carbohydrate, 0.5 fat*

Quick Cranberry Cream Cheese Bubble Ring

Simple and sensational, this tasty creation starts with canned biscuits and ends as an irresistible melt-in-your-mouth treasure.
The first time I made this recipe, my kids thought I had been to the bakery!

MAKES 8 SERVINGS

6 ounces reduced-fat cream cheese, softened
1/2 cup dried cranberries
1/3 cup sugar
11/2 teaspoons grated orange rind
2 (10-biscuit) cans refrigerated biscuits
2 tablespoons margarine, melted
1/4 cup light brown sugar
2 tablespoons chopped pecans, toasted
  (see Terrific Tip below)

Terrific Tip

TO TOAST NUTS, SPREAD THEM OUT ON A BAKING SHEET, AND TRANSFER TO A PREHEATED 325°F OVEN. THE COOKING TIME WILL TAKE BETWEEN 5 AND 10 MINUTES, DEPENDING ON THE TYPE OF NUT. CHECK THE NUTS FREQUENTLY, SHAKING THEM AROUND ON THE BAKING SHEET, AND CHECKING FOR COLOR AND THAT NUTTY, TOASTED SMELL. CHOPPED OR SLICED NUTS WILL TAKE LESS TIME TO COOK THAN WHOLE NUTS.

Preheat the oven to 375°F.

In a mixing bowl, mix together the cream cheese, cranberries, sugar, and orange rind until creamy.

Flatten each biscuit into a circle about 3 inches in diameter. Divide the cream cheese mixture evenly among the 20 flattened biscuits, dolloping some of the mixture on top of each one. Pull up two sides of the biscuit dough, and pinch at the top to seal.

Pour half the melted margarine evenly into a 5-cup ring mold, and sprinkle with half the brown sugar and pecans. Place half the rolled biscuits in the ring mold, seam side up. Pour the remaining margarine over the first layer of biscuits, sprinkle with the remaining sugar and pecans, and top with the remaining biscuits. Bake for 20 to 30 minutes, or until the biscuits are done. Immediately invert the pan onto a serving plate, and serve.

Nutritional Information per Serving
Calories 296, Protein (g) 6, Carbohydrate (g) 46, Fat (g) 10, Calories from Fat (%) 31, Saturated Fat (g) 4, Dietary Fiber (g) 1, Cholesterol (mg) 15, Sodium (mg) 575
Diabetic Exchanges: *2.5 starch, 0.5 fruit, 1.5 fat*

Terrific Tip

TO PREPARE THE QUICK CRANBERRY CREAM CHEESE BUBBLE RING IN ADVANCE, TIGHTLY COVER THE UNBAKED CASSEROLE WITH PLASTIC WRAP, AND STORE IN THE REFRIGERATOR FOR UP TO 4 HOURS. THEN BRING TO ROOM TEMPERATURE BEFORE BAKING AS DIRECTED.

Mocha Coffee Punch

Coffee is a morning ritual for many, but this recipe will add some variety to the daily brew.
Your guests will think they are sipping a decadent drink from a trendy coffee shop! Serve in a punch bowl or from a pitcher,
and offer separate bowls of whipped topping and cocoa for added flair. This recipe will attract all ages and even those
who aren't regular coffee drinkers. If you prefer a spiked version, coffee liqueur may be added.

MAKES 24 TO 30 SERVINGS

2 quarts brewed coffee (flavored or
  decaffeinated coffee may be used),
  cooled to room temperature
1/2 cup chocolate syrup
3/4 cup sugar
1 tablespoon vanilla extract
2 cups skim milk
2 cups fat-free half & half
1 quart fat-free vanilla ice cream
  or vanilla frozen yogurt, softened
1 (8-ounce) container frozen fat-free
  whipped topping, defrosted
Cocoa, for serving

In a large container, add the cooled coffee, chocolate syrup, sugar, and vanilla. Refrigerate until well chilled or overnight.

When ready to serve, in a very large container, combine the coffee mixture, milk, and half & half. Transfer to a punch bowl, and add large spoonfuls of ice cream. Add a dollop of whipped topping to each serving, and sprinkle with cocoa.

Nutritional Information per Serving
Calories 91, Protein (g) 3, Carbohydrate (g) 20, Fat (g) 0, Calories from Fat (%) 0, Saturated Fat (g) 0, Dietary Fiber (g) 0, Cholesterol (mg) 0, Sodium (mg) 50
Diabetic Exchanges: *1.5 other carbohydrate*

STRAWBERRY SMOOTHIES

Strawberry Smoothies

A fruit smoothie starts your day on a naturally sweet note, and it's a super way to get one of your five fruits a day.
If the strawberries aren't sweet, I sometimes add just a little sugar to the mixture.

MAKES 4 SERVINGS

1 pint fresh strawberries, stems removed
  and halved
1 banana
1/2 cup orange juice
1 cup crushed ice

In a food processor or blender, process the strawberries, banana, orange juice, and ice until smooth. Serve immediately.

Nutritional Information per Serving
Calories 63, Protein (g) 0, Carbohydrate (g) 15, Fat (g) 0, Calories from Fat (%) 0,
Saturated Fat (g) 0, Dietary Fiber (g) 2, Cholesterol (mg) 0, Sodium (mg) 1
Diabetic Exchanges: *1 fruit*

Terrific Tip
FROZEN FRUIT WORKS GREAT WHEN MAKING
SMOOTHIES. FREEZE THE BANANA IN ADVANCE
AND IT WILL KEEP THE SMOOTHIE COLDER. PLUS,
YOU CAN KEEP BANANAS ON HAND MUCH LONGER
THAT WAY, FOR SMOOTHIES ANYTIME.

Ladies' Lunch On the Run

We have to meet, and we have to eat! Whether you are hosting a business meeting, a club gathering, or a spontaneous afternoon celebration, a luncheon is the perfect forum for discussion or simply taking a moment to enjoy one another's company. A lighter menu consisting of various salads and innovative appetizers creates an ideal selection for those who don't have much time to spare. With that in mind, I have selected mostly make-ahead recipes for time efficient cooking. For a more formal luncheon, you can serve your creations with small china plates, demitasse cups, trifle dishes, or glass bowls to showcase the wonderful colors and textures of the food. When hosting a more casual lunch, take a fun, creative approach to an afternoon with the girls by using colored containers to serve your salads. I always like to greet my guests with a tray in hand, offering cups of soup (like the delicious Strawberry Orange Soup) to welcome them and encourage mingling while the others arrive. I couldn't decide which salads are my favorites—I love them all—so choose those you like best and share them with your friends and family.

EXCITING EXTRAS

- Serve salads in colored, disposable containers or Chinese food cartons for individual, on-the-go lunches.
- Attractive paper goods and high quality plastic utensils increase the ease of hosting a casual lunch without sacrificing charm.
- Make or buy several kinds of miniature muffins—they're small, so your guests can taste them all!
- Use a collection of different demitasse cups as a lovely way to serve coffee.
- Float strawberries and lemon slices in lemonade for a lovely, refreshing drink.
- Fresh flowers in small vases add a fresh, light, decorative touch that we ladies love.

Short Cuts

▶ Purchase a fresh assortment of salads to round out your menu. You should have no trouble finding options like green salads, chicken salads with fruit, pasta salads, and marinated veggie salads at your local supermarket or deli.

▶ Make Cheese Date Balls ahead of time and freeze.

▶ Select store-bought flavored ice teas, from herb to raspberry, and serve in a pitcher.

▶ Make bar cookies ahead of time and freeze.

Cheese Date Balls

Spicy, crunchy, and sweet sensations entice you to keep popping these wonderful creations in your mouth.
If you make them ahead of time, or if by chance you do have some leftovers, these baked treats may be frozen in plastic storage bags.

MAKES 42 TO 48 BALLS

1½ cups shredded reduced-fat sharp
   Cheddar cheese
1½ cups all-purpose flour
½ cup (1 stick) margarine
2 tablespoons water
¼ teaspoon salt
¼ teaspoon cayenne pepper
1 cup pitted dates, halved
½ cup coarsely chopped walnuts or pecans

Preheat the oven to 400°F. In a food processor, add the cheese, flour, margarine, water, salt, and cayenne, and process until a soft dough is formed. Add more water if necessary to form the dough.

Mold a small amount of dough around a date half with some walnuts, covering the center well to make a small ball with the date-walnut combination hidden inside.

Place the balls on ungreased baking sheets and bake for 15 to 17 minutes, or until the bottom of the balls are light brown. Serve at room temperature.

Nutritional Information per Serving (per ball)
Calories 60, Protein (g) 2, Carbohydrate (g) 6, Fat (g) 3, Calories from Fat (%) 50,
Saturated Fat (g) 1, Dietary Fiber (g) 0, Cholesterol (mg) 2, Sodium (mg) 57
Diabetic Exchanges: *0.5 starch, 0.5 fat*

Gorgonzola Mound with Apple Slices

The unique, pungent cheese, a touch of brandy, and earthy pecans are all perfect compliments
to the mildly tart apples. This easy recipe can also be served with crackers.

MAKES 1 CUP, OR 24 SERVINGS

4 ounces Gorgonzola cheese
4 ounces fat-free cream cheese
2 teaspoons brandy (optional)
¼ cup chopped pecans, toasted
   (see Terrific Tip, page 22)
3 apples, red or green, cored and sliced
   (8 slices per apple)

In a food processor or mixer, beat together the Gorgonzola cheese, cream cheese, and brandy, if desired. Mix in the pecans. On a platter, mound the cheese mixture and surround it with apple slices.

Nutritional Information per Serving
Calories 41, Protein (g) 2, Carbohydrate (g) 3, Fat (g) 2, Calories from Fat (%) 52,
Fat (g) 1, Dietary Fiber (g) 1, Cholesterol (mg) 5, Sodium (mg) 23
Diabetic Exchanges: *0.5 fat*

Terrific Tip
DIP APPLE SLICES IN LEMON JUICE TO KEEP
THEM FROM TURNING BROWN.

Strawberry Orange Soup

A small cup of this refreshing, light, velvety cold soup is perfect for those initial moments of mingling before all the guests arrive. Garnish with mint or strawberries for extra appeal.

MAKES 4 TO 6 SERVINGS

1 pint strawberries, stems removed
1 (12-ounce) can peach nectar
1 orange, squeezed (about ½ cup juice)
3 tablespoons honey
1 tablespoon confectioners' sugar
1 teaspoon grated orange rind
1½ cups nonfat plain yogurt
1 tablespoon orange liqueur (optional)
Fresh strawberries or mint, for garnish

In a food processor or blender, combine the strawberries, peach nectar, orange juice, honey, and confectioners' sugar, and blend until smooth. Add the orange rind and yogurt, mixing well. If desired, add the orange liqueur, and blend. Refrigerate until well chilled. Serve in soup bowls with fresh strawberries or mint sprigs for garnish.

Nutritional Information per Serving
Calories 129, Protein (g) 4, Carbohydrate (g) 29, Fat (g) 0, Calories from Fat (%) 0,
Saturated Fat (g) 0, Dietary Fiber (g) 2, Cholesterol (mg) 1, Sodium (mg) 53
Diabetic Exchanges: *1 fruit, 0.5 skim milk, 0.5 other carbohydrate*

Terrific Tip
DON'T FRET IF YOU DON'T HAVE AN ORANGE FOR WHEN A RECIPE CALLS FOR GRATED ORANGE RIND. GO TO THE SPICE SECTION AND BUY GRATED ORANGE PEEL, WHICH MAY BE SUBSTITUTED IN ANY RECIPE.

Broccoli Salad Medley

An explosion of color and flavor make this nutritional recipe an outstanding lunch option.

MAKES 4 TO 6 SERVINGS

1 pound fresh broccoli florets
1½ cups seedless red grapes, cut in half
½ cup chopped green onions (scallions)
¼ cup golden raisins
¼ cup light mayonnaise
¼ cup fat-free sour cream
2 tablespoons sugar
2 tablespoons white vinegar
⅓ cup chopped walnuts, toasted
  (see Terrific Tip, page 22)

In a large bowl, combine the broccoli, grapes, green onions, and raisins. In a small bowl, mix together the mayonnaise, sour cream, sugar, and vinegar. Toss this dressing with the salad, and add the walnuts. Serve immediately.

Nutritional Information per Serving
Calories 178, Protein (g) 4, Carbohydrate (g) 25, Fat (g) 8, Calories from Fat (%) 39,
Saturated Fat (g) 1, Dietary Fiber (g) 4, Cholesterol (mg) 5, Sodium (mg) 109
Diabetic Exchanges: *1 fruit, 1 vegetable, 0.5 other carbohydrate, 1.5 fat*

Chicken Apricot Salad

Tangy, sweet apricots mixed with chicken in a mustard dressing with toasted almonds and rosemary make this a spectacular salad— one that I cannot stop eating! This is one time that I insist upon using fresh rosemary; it really makes a difference.

MAKES 6 TO 8 SERVINGS

2 pounds boneless, skinless chicken breasts, cooked (see Terrific Tip)
1 cup dried apricots, cut into ¼-inch strips
1 bunch green onions (scallions), sliced
½ cup chopped celery
⅓ cup light mayonnaise
¼ cup honey mustard
2 tablespoons grainy mustard
2 tablespoons lemon juice
2 tablespoons fresh rosemary leaves
⅓ cup sliced almonds, toasted (see Terrific Tip, page 22)

Shred the chicken with a fork and transfer to a large bowl. Add the apricots, green onions, and celery, and stir to combine.

In a small bowl, mix together the mayonnaise, honey mustard, grainy mustard, lemon juice, and rosemary, and add to the chicken mixture. Add the almonds, and carefully mix all ingredients. Refrigerate before serving.

Nutritional Information per Serving
Calories 320, Protein (g) 37, Carbohydrate (g) 19, Fat (g) 10, Calories from Fat (%) 28, Saturated Fat (g) 2, Dietary Fiber (g) 3, Cholesterol (mg) 100, Sodium (mg) 269
Diabetic Exchanges: *3 lean meat, 1 fruit*

Terrific Tip
TO COOK GREAT TASTING CHICKEN, SEASON SKINLESS CHICKEN BREASTS WITH SALT, GARLIC SALT, AND PEPPER. BAKE AT 350°F FOR ABOUT 1 HOUR, OR UNTIL DONE. USE IMMEDIATELY, OR STORE IN THE FREEZER USING ZIPPER-TOP PLASTIC BAGS. YOU'LL THEN HAVE WONDERFULLY SEASONED CHICKEN ON HAND TO ADD TO ANY DISH.

Tortellini, Broccoli, and Asparagus with Vinaigrette Dressing

Looking for a salad with lots of versatility? This is the one for you. You can use whatever kind of stuffed tortellini you prefer and toss in your favorite veggies. The combination of tortellini with broccoli, asparagus, and this light herb dressing is a definite hit.

MAKES 8 SERVINGS

1 (9-ounce) package cheese tortellini
2 cups broccoli florets, steamed to crisp tender
3/4 pound asparagus spears, cut into 2-inch spears and steamed to crisp tender
1/2 cup chopped green onions (scallions)
1 tablespoon grated Parmesan cheese
1/4 cup olive oil
3 tablespoons white vinegar
2 tablespoons minced fresh parsley
1 teaspoon dried thyme leaves
1 teaspoon dried basil leaves
1/2 teaspoon minced garlic
Salt and pepper, to taste

Cook the tortellini according to the package directions and drain. In a large bowl, mix together the tortellini, broccoli, asparagus, green onions, and Parmesan cheese.

In a small bowl, whisk together the oil, vinegar, parsley, thyme, basil, and garlic. Toss the dressing with the tortellini salad. Add salt and pepper. Refrigerate until ready to serve.

Nutritional Information per Serving
*Calories 121, Protein (g) 4, Carbohydrate (g) 12, Fat (g) 7, Calories from Fat (%) 48,
Saturated Fat (g) 2, Dietary Fiber (g) 2, Cholesterol (mg) 10, Sodium (mg) 91*
Diabetic Exchanges: *1 starch, 1 fat*

Crunchy Coleslaw

My daughter Courtney insisted I create a healthier coleslaw recipe, and we both love the result. You'll see why when you taste this remarkable creation full of fabulous ingredients that takes only minutes to prepare. You can also toss in grilled chicken for a heartier version.

MAKES 8 TO 10 SERVINGS

3 tablespoons olive oil
1/4 cup white wine vinegar
1/4 cup sugar
2 (3-ounce) packages oriental-flavored ramen noodles
1/2 cup slivered almonds
1/4 cup sunflower seeds
8 cups shredded green cabbage
1/2 cup sliced green onions (scallions)

Preheat the oven to 400°F.

To prepare the dressing, in a mixing bowl, whisk together the oil, vinegar, sugar, and the seasoning packets from the ramen noodles. Refrigerate until ready to use.

Break the ramen noodles into pieces, and place them on a baking sheet with the almonds and sunflower seeds. Bake, watching closely, until the noodles, almonds, and sunflower seeds turn light brown, 5 to 7 minutes. Set aside and cool.

In a large bowl, mix the cabbage, green onions, and baked noodles and nut mixture with the dressing. Serve immediately.

Nutritional Information per Serving
*Calories 191, Protein (g) 4, Carbohydrate (g) 21, Fat (g) 11, Calories from Fat (%) 50,
Saturated Fat (g) 3, Dietary Fiber (g) 3, Cholesterol (mg) 0, Sodium (mg) 323*
Diabetic Exchanges: *1 starch, 1 vegetable, 2 fat*

Fruity Bran Muffins

This is truly the ultimate muffin—healthy, flavorful, and easy. You can keep the batter in the refrigerator for up to 4 to 5 days, and bake hot muffins at a moment's notice.

MAKES 48 MUFFINS

1 (15-ounce) box raisin bran cereal
5 cups all-purpose flour
2 cups assorted dried fruits
  (cranberries, apricots, fruit medley)
1 cup sugar
2/3 cup light brown sugar
5 teaspoons baking soda
1 tablespoon ground cinnamon
4 cups buttermilk
4 eggs
1 egg white
1/2 cup canola oil

Preheat the oven to 400°F. Coat a muffin pan with nonstick cooking spray, or line with papers.

In a large bowl, mix together the cereal, flour, dried fruits, sugar, brown sugar, baking soda, and cinnamon. In another bowl, whisk together the buttermilk, eggs, egg white, and oil; add to the cereal mixture, stirring just until moistened.

Spoon the batter into the prepared muffin tins about three-quarters full. Bake for 15 to 17 minutes, or until golden. Let cool in the tins for 5 minutes at room temperature, then turn out onto a wire rack.

Nutritional Information per Serving (per muffin)
Calories 154, Protein (g) 3, Carbohydrate (g) 29, Fat (g) 3, Calories from Fat (%) 19, Saturated Fat (g) 1, Dietary Fiber (g) 2, Cholesterol (mg) 19, Sodium (mg) 199
Diabetic Exchanges: *1.5 starch, 0.5 fruit, 0.5 fat*

Raspberry Coconut Bars

Raspberry and coconut pair together to create this especially elegant bar cookie. This recipe is an easy-to-make sensation, and I have a special fondness for it.

MAKES 60 BARS

1 (18.25-ounce) box yellow cake mix
1/2 cup (1 stick) margarine,
  softened and divided
4 eggs, divided
1 (10-ounce) jar seedless raspberry
  spreadable fruit
1 cup sugar
1/4 teaspoon baking powder
1 teaspoon coconut extract
1/2 cup flaked coconut

Preheat the oven to 350°F. Coat a 15 x 10 x 1-inch baking pan with nonstick cooking spray.

In a mixing bowl, mix together the cake mix, 6 tablespoons of the margarine, and 1 egg until crumbly and mixed. Pat the mixture into the bottom of the prepared baking pan. Bake for 10 minutes. Remove the crust from the oven and carefully spread with the raspberry fruit.

In a mixing bowl, beat together the remaining 3 eggs, the remaining 2 tablespoons of margarine, the sugar, baking powder, and coconut extract. Stir in the flaked coconut, and pour over the raspberry layer. Return the baking pan to the oven, and bake for 15 to 20 minutes, or until the filling is set. Cool completely at room temperature before serving.

Nutritional Information per Serving (per bar)
Calories 80, Protein (g) 1, Carbohydrate (g) 3, Fat (g) 3, Calories from Fat (%) 32, Saturated Fat (g) 1, Dietary Fiber (g) 0, Cholesterol (mg) 14, Sodium (mg) 86
Diabetic Exchanges: *1 other carbohydrate, 1/2 fat*

Terrific Tip

PURCHASE A CAN OF FROZEN RASPBERRY LEMONADE IN THE FREEZER SECTION, MAKE ACCORDING TO THE DIRECTIONS, AND SERVE IN PITCHER FOR A REFRESHING DRINK.

RASPBERRY COCONUT BARS and
CHOCOLATE, RAISIN, AND PEANUT BARS

Chocolate, Raisin, and Peanut Bars

*The sweet-and-salty flavor of the peanuts coated with rich chocolate makes this one of the best bar cookies ever.
After one taste, I'm sure you'll agree.*

MAKES 48 BARS

2/3 cup sugar
1/2 cup (1 stick) margarine, softened
1/3 cup dark corn syrup
1 teaspoon vanilla extract
2 cups all-purpose flour
1 cup semisweet chocolate chips
2/3 cup raisins
2/3 cup peanuts
1/3 cup reduced-fat creamy peanut butter

Preheat the oven to 350°F. Coat a 13 x 9 x 2-inch baking pan with nonstick cooking spray.

In a mixing bowl, mix together the sugar, margarine, corn syrup, and vanilla. Add the flour, and mix just until combined. Pat the dough into the prepared baking pan, and bake for 18 to 22 minutes, or until golden brown. Set the pan on a wire rack to cool.

In a medium pot over low heat (or in a microwaveable dish in the microwave oven), heat the chocolate chips, raisins, peanuts, and peanut butter, stirring, until melted. Spread over the cooked crust. Refrigerate for 1 hour before cutting.

Nutritional Information per Serving (per bar)
*Calories 99, Protein (g) 2, Carbohydrate (g) 14, Fat (g) 5, Calories from Fat (%) 40,
Saturated Fat (g) 1, Dietary Fiber (g) 1, Cholesterol (mg) 0, Sodium (mg) 41*
Diabetic Exchanges: *1 other carbohydrate, 1 fat*

Lemon Custard Bars

This recipe transforms luscious, tart, lemon custard pie into a spectacular bar cookie. There are a few steps, but it's worth the effort!

MAKES 30 TO 36 BARS

½ cup (1 stick) margarine, softened
½ cup light brown sugar
1½ cups all-purpose flour
3 teaspoons grated lemon rind, divided
1½ cups sugar, divided
½ cup lemon juice
½ cup water
2 tablespoons cornstarch
2 eggs

Preheat the oven to 350°F. Coat a 9 x 9 x 2-inch pan with nonstick cooking spray.

To make the crust, in a large bowl, beat together the margarine and brown sugar until light and fluffy. Add the flour and 1 teaspoon of the lemon rind, mixing just until combined. Pat the mixture into the prepared baking pan. Bake for 15 minutes. Set the pan on a wire rack to cool.

Meanwhile, in a 2-quart pot, mix together 1 cup of the sugar with the lemon juice, water, and cornstarch. Heat the mixture to boiling over medium heat, stirring constantly. Continue cooking, stirring, until the mixture thickens, 1 to 2 minutes. Remove from the heat.

In a medium bowl, whisk together the remaining ½ cup of sugar, the remaining 2 teaspoons of lemon rind, and the eggs, until thick and lemon-colored. Slowly beat the warm lemon mixture into the egg mixture until well combined. Pour the filling onto the prepared crust. Continue baking for 15 to 20 minutes, or until the filling is firm. Cool to room temperature on a wire rack before cutting.

Nutritional Information per Serving (per bar)
Calories 92, Protein (g) 1, Carbohydrate (g) 16, Fat (g) 3, Calories from Fat (%) 27, Saturated Fat (g) 1, Dietary Fiber (g) 0, Cholesterol (mg) 12, Sodium (mg) 35
Diabetic Exchanges: *1 other carbohydrate, 0.5 fat*

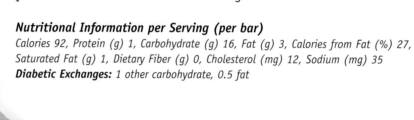

Tropical Paradise Party

I love the late sunsets and long, breezy evenings of spring and summer, and I always enjoy outdoor entertaining during that carefree time of year. I have a lush, open backyard that creates the perfect atmosphere for a tropical theme party. Wherever the gathering, exotic fruits, bright colors, and interesting flavors create a fun, tropical feel. Whether you are celebrating a graduation, having an office party, or just welcoming an end to the winter blues, attaching a theme to your soiree not only adds pizzazz but also makes decorating and menu planning much easier. Any occasion is enhanced when you serve Chicken Kebobs, Paradise Couscous Salad, and, of course, strawberry daiquiris (see Terrific Tip, page 41). A culinary trip to the tropics appeals to guests of all ages, and there's no better way to take advantage of the bounty of the warm season. While the blender is running and the appetizers are disappearing into eager mouths, you can man the grill yourself or assign that responsibility to one of your eager-to-help guests. Chicken, beef, and an array of vegetables give you ample grilling options that are sure to please any crowd. Aloha!

MENU SELECTIONS

EXCITING EXTRAS

- Put little umbrellas from the party store in drinks.
- Hollow out different colored bell peppers to use as containers for dips, sauces, or even flowers.
- Have flowered leis on the table for everyone, or greet each of your guests at the door with a lei.
- Use a pineapple for serving—spike kebobs into the pineapple for a dramatic presentation.

- Purchase pre-made shish kebobs from your local supermarket.
- Use a bottled marinade for the chicken and meat.
- Pick up pre-made frozen drinks—just add alcohol (if desired), and serve.
- Use wooden skewers instead of metal ones for easy handling and easy serving.

Brie and Mango Quesadillas

This is a trendy version of a classic favorite. Onions and chiles, partnered with the sweetness of mango, create a flavor sensation!

MAKES 24 WEDGES

1/2 cup chopped red onion
1 (4-ounce) can diced green chiles
12 (6-inch) flour tortillas
8 ounces Brie, rind removed and diced
1 cup chopped mango
1/2 cup chopped green onions (scallions)

Preheat the oven to 425°F. Coat a baking sheet with nonstick cooking spray.

Coat a skillet with nonstick cooking spray, and set over medium heat. Add the onion and cook, stirring, until tender, about 5 minutes. Remove from the heat, and stir in the green chiles.

Arrange 6 of the tortillas on the prepared baking sheet. Divide equally the Brie, mango, red onion mixture, and green onions on top of the tortillas. Top each with another tortilla, pressing to adhere. Bake the quesadillas for 6 to 8 minutes, or until the cheese melts and the filling is heated. To serve, use a pizza cutter to cut into wedges.

Nutritional Information per Serving (per wedge)
Calories 86, Protein (g) 3, Carbohydrate (g) 10, Fat (g) 4, Calories from Fat (%) 38, Saturated Fat (g) 2, Dietary Fiber (g) 1, Cholesterol (mg) 9, Sodium (mg) 147
Diabetic Exchanges: *0.5 starch, 1 fat*

Chutney and Shrimp Cheese Spread

*I highly recommend this unusual and incredible spread! I predict it will earn a place high on your list of favorite recipes.
Be sure to use a spicy fruit chutney, as it is the perfect compliment to the sweet raisins, curry, and shrimp.
Almonds and coconut provide the grand finale. If desired, the shrimp may be omitted. Serve with crackers or gingersnaps.*

MAKES 20 (2-TABLESPOON) SERVINGS

1 (8-ounce) package reduced-fat cream cheese, softened
3 tablespoons fat-free sour cream
1 teaspoon curry powder
1/2 cup sliced green onions (scallions)
1/2 cup golden raisins
1 cup cooked small, peeled shrimp (see Terrific Tip)
1/2 cup spicy mango chutney, or another spicy fruit variety
2 tablespoons sliced almonds, toasted (see Terrific Tip, page 22)
2 tablespoons flaked coconut, toasted (see Terrific Tip)

In a medium bowl, stir together the cream cheese, sour cream, and curry powder until smooth. Stir in the green onions, raisins, and shrimp. Flatten into a round disk and spread the top with chutney. Sprinkle the top with the almonds and coconut. Refrigerate until ready to serve.

Nutritional Information per Serving
Calories 76, Protein (g) 3, Carbohydrate (g) 9, Fat (g) 3, Calories from Fat (%) 37, Saturated Fat (g) 2, Dietary Fiber (g) 1, Cholesterol (mg) 21, Sodium (mg) 69
Diabetic Exchanges: *0.5 fruit, 0.5 fat*

Terrific Tip
PICK UP SMALL, PEELED SHRIMP FROM YOUR LOCAL SUPERMARKET FOR ONE-STOP SHOPPING. TO COOK THE SHRIMP, SAUTÉ THEM USING MARGARINE OR NONSTICK COOKING SPRAY, AND SEASON TO TASTE.

Terrific Tip
TO TOAST FLAKED COCONUT, SPREAD COCONUT ON A BAKING SHEET AND PLACE IN A PREHEATED 350° OVEN FOR 5 MINUTES, STIRRING AFTER 3 MINUTES, OR UNTIL LIGHTLY BROWNED.

Black Bean, Corn, and Avocado Salsa

There are no fussy details to complicate this alluring, colorful dip. Full of flavor and texture,
you will find yourself turning to this quick appetizer for all occasions. Serve with chips.

MAKES 24 (¼-CUP) SERVINGS

1 (15-ounce) can black beans,
  rinsed and drained
1½ cups frozen corn or 1 (11-ounce)
  can corn, drained
1 cup cherry tomatoes, cut in half
1 bunch green onions (scallions), sliced
⅓ cup chopped red onion
1 avocado, diced
½ teaspoon minced garlic
2 tablespoons lime juice
1 tablespoon lemon juice
1 tablespoon olive oil
1 teaspoon ground cumin
1 teaspoon chili powder
Lots of salt and pepper

In a large bowl, mix together the black beans, corn, tomatoes, green onions, red onion, avocado, and garlic. In a small bowl, whisk together the lime juice, lemon juice, olive oil, cumin, and chili powder. Toss the dressing with the black bean mixture. Season to taste with salt and pepper, and refrigerate until ready to serve.

Nutritional Information per Serving
Calories 48, Protein (g) 2, Carbohydrate (g) 6, Fat (g) 2,
Calories from Fat (%) 37, Saturated Fat (g) 0, Dietary Fiber (g) 2,
Cholesterol (mg) 0, Sodium (mg) 58
Diabetic Exchanges: *0.5 starch, 0.5 fat*

Terrific Tip
USE VINE-RIPENED CHERRY TOMATOES FOR
THAT HOME-GROWN FLAVOR YEAR ROUND.

Steak on a Stick

Our friend Katie gave me this recipe, and my kids request this fun entrée all the time. Marinade the steak the night before
in these rich, wonderful ingredients and grill for only minutes for meat that melts in your mouth.

MAKES 30 TO 36 SKEWERS

2 pounds flank steak
1 (10¾-ounce) can beef consommé
1 cup red wine
½ cup reduced-sodium soy sauce
⅓ cup lime juice
¼ cup honey
1 tablespoon minced garlic

Trim any excess fat from the flank steak. Slice the flank steak into thin strips, across the grain, about ½ inch wide. In a shallow glass dish, mix together the beef consommé, red wine, soy sauce, lime juice, honey, and garlic. Add the flank steak strips and marinate for several hours or overnight if time permits.

When ready to serve, prepare a medium-hot grill. Thread the steak strips onto wooden bamboo skewers. Grill for 5 to 10 minutes, turning half way through, watching carefully to prevent overcooking.

Nutritional Information per Serving (per skewer)
Calories 42, Protein (g) 5, Carbohydrate (g) 0, Fat (g) 2, Calories from Fat (%) 41,
Saturated Fat (g) 1, Dietary Fiber (g) 0, Cholesterol (mg) 12, Sodium (mg) 145
Diabetic Exchanges: *0.5 lean meat*

Terrific Tip
TAKE ADVANTAGE OF SEASONAL FRUITS AND VEGETABLES
BY USING THEM AS SERVING PIECES. I LOVE TO STICK
MY KEBOBS IN A PINEAPPLE AND USE HOLLOWED-OUT
COLORED PEPPERS TO SERVE DIPS OR HOLD FLOWERS.

Potato and Pepper Kebobs

Sweet potatoes, potatoes, and peppers add a spectrum of colors and nutrients. Spearing ingredients on skewers is a fun way to serve veggies, tropical style.

MAKES 8 SKEWERS

1¹/₂ pounds sweet potatoes (yams)

1 pound small white potatoes

¹/₄ cup olive oil

2 tablespoons minced fresh parsley

¹/₄ teaspoon cayenne pepper

Salt and pepper, to taste

1 red bell pepper, cored and cut into chunks

1 green bell pepper, cored and cut into chunks

Peel the sweet and white potatoes, and cut into 2-inch chunks. Place the potato chunks in a 2-quart casserole dish along with ¹/₂ cup water. Cover and microwave for 12 to 15 minutes, or until the potatoes are almost done; drain.

In a small bowl, whisk together the olive oil, parsley, cayenne, salt, and pepper. Pour over the potatoes, mixing to coat. Thread the potatoes and bell peppers onto skewers, alternating between sweet and white potatoes and colored peppers.

When ready to serve, prepare a medium-hot grill. Grill the kebobs, turning frequently, for 15 to 20 minutes, or until a nice brown crust forms.

Nutritional Information per Serving (per skewer)
Calories 177, Protein (g) 3, Carbohydrate (g) 34, Fat (g) 5, Calories from Fat (%) 24, Saturated Fat (g) 1, Dietary Fiber (g) 4, Cholesterol (mg) 0, Sodium (mg) 31
Diabetic Exchanges: *2 starch, 0.5 fat*

Terrific Tip

INSTEAD OF METAL SKEWERS, TRY USING BAMBOO SKEWERS FOR YOUR KEBOBS.

Chicken Kebobs

A fruity marinade with a kick seasons this chicken dish. Use this recipe for inspiration, and add your favorite vegetables to the skewers. I especially love the grilled pineapple.

MAKES 8 SKEWERS

2 pounds boneless, skinless chicken breasts
1½ cups pineapple juice
¼ cup reduced-sodium soy sauce
1 tablespoon minced garlic
1 teaspoon ground ginger
1 green bell pepper, cored and cut into chunks
1 onion, cut into chunks
1 pineapple, cut into chunks
½ pound fresh mushrooms
1 pint cherry tomatoes

Trim any excess fat from the chicken and cut into 1-inch chunks. In a 2-quart glass dish, mix together the pineapple juice, soy sauce, garlic, and ginger. Stir in the chicken chunks, cover, and refrigerate for several hours or overnight.

When ready to serve, prepare a medium-hot grill. Discard the marinade. Thread the chicken, bell pepper, onion, pineapple, mushrooms, and tomatoes, on the skewers, without crowding the pieces together. Grill for about 15 to 20 minutes, or until the meat is cooked through, turning half way through the cooking time.

Nutritional Information per Serving (per skewer)
Calories 191, Protein (g) 29, Carbohydrate (g) 15, Fat (g) 2, Calories from Fat (%) 9, Saturated Fat (g) 0, Dietary Fiber (g) 2, Cholesterol (mg) 66, Sodium (mg) 277
Diabetic Exchanges: *3 very lean meat, 0.5 fruit, 1.5 vegetable*

Paradise Couscous Salad

The toasty pecans, along with fresh oranges, tart cranberries, and spinach, highlight this incredible yet easy-to-prepare salad.

MAKES 8 SERVINGS

1 cup orange juice
1 cup water
1 teaspoon olive oil
2 cups couscous
2 cups fresh orange sections
1 cup packed baby spinach
½ cup chopped red bell pepper
½ cup chopped red onion
⅓ cup dried cranberries
⅓ cup coarsely chopped pecans
½ teaspoon sugar
⅛ teaspoon cayenne pepper
Apricot Vinaigrette (recipe follows)

APRICOT VINAIGRETTE:
⅓ cup apricot nectar
⅓ cup red wine vinegar
2 tablespoons sugar
1 tablespoon olive oil
2 teaspoons Dijon mustard

In a medium pot, bring the orange juice, water, and olive oil to a boil. Stir in the couscous, cover, remove from the heat, and let stand for 7 minutes. Transfer to a large bowl, and fluff with a fork. Add the orange sections, spinach, bell pepper, onion, and cranberries, mixing well.

In a small nonstick skillet over medium heat, add the pecans. Sprinkle with the sugar and cayenne, and cook, stirring frequently, for until pecans begin to brown, 5 to 7 minutes. Remove from the heat to cool, and set aside. Before serving, toss the couscous mixture with the Apricot Vinaigrette. Toss with the sugared pecans. Refrigerate until ready to serve.

Apricot Vinaigrette: In a small bowl, whisk together the apricot nectar, vinegar, sugar, olive oil, and mustard.

Nutritional Information per Serving
Calories 339, Protein (g) 9, Carbohydrate (g) 61, Fat (g) 7, Calories from Fat (%) 18, Saturated Fat (g) 1, Dietary Fiber (g) 4, Cholesterol (mg) 0, Sodium (mg) 38
Diabetic Exchanges: *3 starch, 1 fruit, 1 fat*

Terrific Tip
VASES AREN'T THE ONLY VESSELS FOR FLOWERS! SIMPLY LAYING EXOTIC TROPICAL FLOWERS IN A BASKET ENHANCES THE TABLE DECOR.

Yam Trifle

Easy and elegant! Yes, sweet potatoes are the star ingredients in this sensational dessert. I love trifles because they serve (and impress) a crowd and can be made ahead of time.

MAKES 12 TO 16 SERVINGS

12 ounces reduced-fat cream cheese, softened

3/4 cup sugar, divided

1 (5-ounce) can fat-free evaporated milk

1 teaspoon coconut extract

1 (16-ounce) store-bought angel food cake, cut into cubes

2 (15-ounce) cans sweet potatoes (yams), drained and mashed, or 2 cups fresh sweet potatoes, cooked and mashed

1/2 teaspoon vanilla extract

2 tablespoons flaked coconut, divided

1 (8-ounce) container frozen fat-free whipped topping, thawed

1 tablespoon flaked coconut, toasted (see Terrific Tip, page 36)

1 tablespoon chopped pecans, toasted (see Terrific Tip, page 22)

In a large bowl, beat together the cream cheese and 1/2 cup of the sugar. Gradually add the evaporated milk and coconut extract, mixing until creamy. Fold the cubed angel food cake into the cream cheese mixture, and set aside.

In another bowl, beat together the yams, the remaining 1/4 cup of sugar, and the vanilla until creamy.

In a trifle bowl or large glass bowl, layer half the angel food cake mixture, half the yam mixture, 1 tablespoon of the coconut, and half the whipped topping. Repeat the layers. Sprinkle the top with the toasted coconut and pecans. Refrigerate until well chilled, and serve.

Nutritional Information per Serving
Calories 257, Protein (g) 6, Carbohydrate (g) 45, Fat (g) 6,
Calories from Fat (%) 20, Saturated Fat (g) 4,
Dietary Fiber (g) 1, Cholesterol (mg) 16, Sodium (mg) 298
Diabetic Exchanges: *1 starch, 2 other carbohydrate, 1 fat*

Terrific Tip
SWEET POTATOES FROM LOUISIANA ARE REFERRED TO AS "YAMS." LOUISIANA OFFERS IDEAL SOIL AND CLIMATE CONDITIONS TO GROW THEM.

Lemon Angel Food Cake Bars

This dessert is simple and heavenly with a light lemon flavor, a tropical hint of coconut, and a divine cream cheese icing.

MAKES 48 TO 60 BARS

1 (16-ounce) package angel food cake mix

1 (22-ounce) can lemon pie filling

1/2 cup flaked coconut

6 ounces reduced-fat cream cheese, softened

2 tablespoons margarine, softened

1 (16-ounce) box confectioners' sugar

1/2 teaspoon coconut extract

1/2 teaspoon vanilla extract

Preheat the oven to 350°F. Coat a 15 x 10 x 1-inch baking pan with nonstick cooking spray.

In a mixing bowl, stir together the cake mix, lemon pie filling, and coconut until thoroughly mixed. Spread the mixture in the prepared baking pan. Bake for 15 to 20 minutes, or until toothpick inserted in center comes out clean. Cool completely.

In a mixing bowl, beat together the cream cheese and margarine until creamy. Mix in the confectioners' sugar, coconut extract, and vanilla, mixing until smooth. Carefully spread the icing on the cooled cake, cut into bars, and serve.

Nutritional Information per Serving (per bar)
Calories 88, Protein (g) 1, Carbohydrate (g) 18, Fat (g) 2, Calories from Fat (%) 16,
Saturated Fat (g) 1, Dietary Fiber (g) 0, Cholesterol (mg) 2, Sodium (mg) 89
Diabetic Exchanges: *1 other carbohydrate*

41

Terrific Tip

WHEN YOU CAN'T DECIDE IF YOU WANT A STRAWBERRY DAIQUIRI OR A PIÑA COLODA, HAVE THEM BOTH BY LAYERING THEM IN TALL GLASSES. ALCOHOLIC OR NONALCOHOLIC, THEY ARE PRETTY TO LOOK AT AND EVEN MORE FUN TO DRINK. YOU CAN PURCHASE DIFFERENT DAIQUIRI MIXES IN THE FREEZER SECTION OF THE SUPERMARKET.

The Big Enchilada

Those who are familiar with my party-planning ways will tell you that I am partial to a Southwestern theme. My husband's surprise birthday party (his age is a secret!) and the multitude of engagement celebrations I have held at my home have all ended up with a Southwestern flair. Mexican food is typically less expensive than other options, and it efficiently serves a crowd while encouraging a spicy good time. Salsa, guacamole, and chips are a must, but try my extraordinary baked Savory Southwestern Cheesecake for a unique addition to a traditional menu. Serve an abundance of appetizers with the fajitas and enchiladas that comprise the meal. I think the term "grazing" must have originated with Southwestern food as I can't stop myself from continuously nibbling on these wonderful dips and sauces. There is no need for an extensive open bar as margaritas, beer, and wine can keep the bar tab down. A selection of colorful veggies, piñatas, and sombreros make festive table decorations, and therefore you'll need very few flowers. However, if sunflowers are available, I love to spread them around to brighten the atmosphere. So whenever you find yourself to be the designated hostess, throw a Southwestern fiesta for a casual, pleasurable evening with minimal effort and unlimited options.

MENU SELECTIONS

EXCITING EXTRAS

▶ Instead of flowers, use peppers, eggplant, chilies, cherry tomatoes, and assorted colored vegetables for table decorations.

▶ Decorate with piñatas and sombreros to accent your Southwestern theme.

▶ Rent a margarita machine when entertaining a large crowd.

▶ Purchase cocktail napkins in different bold, bright colors or decorated with a Southwestern design.

▶ When making homemade chips, use tortillas of a variety of flavors and colors.

▶ Float oranges in a pitcher of Simple Sangria Punch (see Terrific Tip, page 44).

Short Cuts

▶ Pick up pre-made chips
  and salsa from your favorite
  local Mexican restaurant.
▶ Serve only fajitas, and
  offer chicken and beef.
▶ Prepare the enchiladas
  ahead of time and freeze.
▶ Purchase pralines from
  a gourmet candy shop.

CHUNKY GUACAMOLE, FRESH & QUICK SALSA, and HOMEMADE TORTILLA CHIPS

SALSA BAR

A salsa bar is a fun way to highlight different salsas and chips. After all, when we go out for Mexican food,
I think we all love chips and salsa the best! If you come up with any other dips and salsas to add to the salsa bar, go ahead.
I always make plenty of the classic Fresh & Quick Salsa, because it's everyone's favorite.

Terrific Tip
TO MAKE SIMPLE SANGRIA PUNCH: IN A LARGE
PITCHER, MIX TOGETHER 1 QUART CRANBERRY JUICE,
2 CUPS GRAPE JUICE, THE JUICE OF 2 LEMONS, AND
THE JUICE OF 1 LIME. GARNISH WITH ORANGE SLICES,
FILL WITH ICE, AND SERVE.

Fresh & Quick Salsa

This simple salsa might seem intimidating with all its fresh ingredients, but everything just goes in the food processor and it's ready in a flash. When juicy summer tomatoes are at their peak, this recipe is hard to beat. It's great with fresh cilantro, too.

MAKES 24 (¼-CUP) SERVINGS

4 tomatoes, cored and cut into chunks
1 tablespoon chopped garlic
1 onion, cut in chunks
1 green bell pepper, cored and cut
 into chunks
1 to 2 jalapeño peppers, cut into pieces
1 tablespoon lime juice
1 teaspoon dried oregano leaves
Salt and pepper, to taste

Place 1 tomato in a food processor and purée with the garlic. Add the onion, bell pepper, jalapeño peppers, lime juice, and oregano, and pulse the processor to coarsely chop. Add the remaining tomatoes, and pulse to coarsely chop. Add salt and pepper to taste.

Nutritional Information per Serving
Calories 11, Protein (g) 0, Carbohydrate (g) 3, Fat (g) 0, Calories from Fat (%) 0, Saturated Fat (g) 0, Dietary Fiber (g) 1, Cholesterol (mg) 0, Sodium (mg) 3
Diabetic Exchanges: *Free*

Pineapple Mango Salsa

For convenience or if fresh fruit is not available, canned pineapple and mango may be used in this fruity variation of classic salsa. This salsa is also a wonderful compliment to fish.

MAKES 10 (¼-CUP) SERVINGS

1 cup cubed mango
1 cup cubed pineapple
½ cup chopped red onion
2 tablespoons orange juice
1 tablespoon lime juice
1 tablespoon chopped fresh cilantro
1 teaspoon finely chopped pickled
 jalapeño peppers
1 teaspoon sugar
Salt and pepper, to taste

In a medium nonreactive bowl (such as glass or plastic), mix together the mango, pineapple, red onion, orange juice, lime juice, cilantro, jalapeño peppers, sugar, salt, and pepper. Refrigerate until ready to serve.

Nutritional Information per Serving
Calories 25, Protein (g) 0, Carbohydrate (g) 6, Fat (g) 0, Calories from Fat (%) 0, Saturated, Fat (g) 0, Dietary Fiber (g) 1, Cholesterol (mg) 0, Sodium (mg) 1
Diabetic Exchanges: *0.5 fruit*

Terrific Tip
THERE ARE THREE COMPONENTS TO THE PERFECT SALSA:
▸ SWEET—FRUIT OR TOMATO
▸ HEAT—CHILE PEPPERS LIKE SERRANO OR JALAPEÑO
▸ ACIDITY—LIME JUICE

Homemade Tortilla Chips

These chips are not much trouble to make but so much better than those you purchase in stores.

Tortillas
Nonstick olive oil spray
Coarse salt

Preheat the oven to 375°F. Use a pizza wheel to cut the tortillas into strips and triangles. Spray with the olive oil cooking spray or brush with olive oil, and sprinkle with the coarse salt. Bake for 5 to 7 minutes. Serve warm, or cool to room temperature.

Terrific Tip
USE DIFFERENT COLORED AND FLAVORED TORTILLAS, SUCH AS THE PESTO OR ROASTED TOMATO VARIETIES. THE DIVERSE COLOR WILL ADD TO THE FESTIVITY OF YOUR TABLE SETTING.

Nutritional Information per Serving (per one 6-inch flour tortilla)
Calories 85, Protein (g) 2, Carbohydrate (g) 18, Fat (g) 0, Calories from Fat (%) 0, Saturated Fat (g) 0, Dietary Fiber (g) 1, Cholesterol (mg) 0, Sodium (mg) 262
Diabetic Exchanges: *1 starch*

Mexican Bean Dip

If you've been looking for a great tasting bean dip recipe, this one wins the prize.

MAKES 24 (2-TABLESPOON) SERVINGS

1 (15-ounce) can pinto beans, rinsed and drained
1/4 cup chopped onion
1/2 teaspoon minced garlic
1 teaspoon chili powder
1/2 teaspoon ground cumin
1 cup chopped avocado
1 cup chopped tomatoes
1/3 cup salsa
2 tablespoons chopped pickled jalapeño peppers
1 tablespoon lemon juice
Salt and pepper, to taste

Process the beans in a food processor until smooth. Add the onion, garlic, chili powder, and cumin, and pulse the food processor until smooth. Transfer to a mixing bowl, and mix in the avocado, tomatoes, salsa, jalapeño peppers, lemon juice, salt, and pepper. Refrigerate until ready to serve.

Nutritional Information per Serving
Calories 29, Protein (g) 1, Carbohydrate (g) 4, Fat (g) 1, Calories from Fat (%) 35, Saturated Fat (g) 0, Dietary Fiber (g) 1, Cholesterol (mg) 0, Sodium (mg) 61
Diabetic Exchanges: *1 vegetable*

Terrific Tip
USE A VARIETY OF CASUAL, EARTHY SERVING PIECES TO GIVE A SOUTHWESTERN FEEL TO YOUR PARTY.

Chunky Guacamole

With tons of texture and flavor from fresh ingredients, this popular Southwestern appetizer disappears quickly, so make lots. It's a good thing that this recipe doubles so easily.

MAKES 12 (2-TABLESPOON) SERVINGS

2 avocados, peeled, pitted, and coarsely mashed
1/3 cup chopped tomatoes
1/4 cup chopped onion
2 tablespoons lime juice
1 tablespoon minced jalapeño peppers
1/2 teaspoon minced garlic
Salt and pepper, to taste

In a medium bowl, combine the avocados, tomatoes, onion, lime juice, jalapeño peppers, garlic, salt, and pepper. Refrigerate until ready to serve.

Nutritional Information per Serving
Calories 57, Protein (g) 1, Carbohydrate (g) 3, Fat (g) 5, Calories from Fat (%) 74, Saturated Fat (g) 1, Dietary Fiber (g) 2, Cholesterol (mg) 0, Sodium (mg) 16
Diabetic Exchanges: *1 fat*

Chicken and Corn Enchiladas

Use flavored tortillas to add color and kick the taste up a notch. For convenience, prepare these enchiladas ahead of time, refrigerate or freeze them until ready to serve, then bake as directed. Because this recipe makes a lot of enchiladas, I usually freeze a pan-full for dinner another night.

MAKES 16 ENCHILADAS

4 cups shredded cooked chicken breasts
(about 2 pounds skinless, boneless
chicken breasts, see Terrific Tip, page 28)

1½ cups chopped red onions

1 (16-ounce) package frozen corn

2 cups shredded reduced-fat
Monterey Jack cheese, divided

1 cup fat-free sour cream

1 teaspoon ground cumin

1 teaspoon chili powder

Salt and pepper, to taste

2 cups mild salsa

3 cups canned enchilada sauce

16 (8-inch) flour tortillas

1 bunch green onions (scallions),
thinly sliced

Preheat the oven to 350°F. Coat two 13 x 9 x 2-inch baking dishes with nonstick cooking spray.

In a large bowl, mix together the chicken, red onions, corn, 1 cup of the cheese, the sour cream, cumin, and chili powder. Season with salt and pepper. In another large bowl, mix together the salsa and enchilada sauce.

Coat a medium skillet with nonstick cooking spray, and set over high heat. Add 1 tortilla to the skillet, and heat for about 10 seconds per side to soften. Spoon a heaping ⅓ cup of the chicken filling into the center of the tortilla. Roll up and place seam side down in a prepared baking dish. Repeat with the remaining tortillas.

Spoon the salsa-enchilada sauce mixture over the filled enchiladas. Sprinkle with the remaining 1 cup of cheese. Cover the baking dishes with foil, and bake for 30 to 40 minutes, until heated through. Uncover, sprinkle with the green onions, and serve immediately.

Nutritional Information per Serving (per enchilada)
Calories 297, Protein (g) 21, Carbohydrate (g) 39, Fat (g) 6, Calories from Fat (%) 17,
Saturated Fat (g) 2, Dietary Fiber (g) 4, Cholesterol (mg) 37, Sodium (mg) 720
Diabetic Exchanges: *2 lean meat, 2.5 starch*

Beef Fajitas

The marinade infuses the meat with Mexican flavor. Serve on a platter with warm tortillas and the other accompaniments. This recipe is always a favorite among all ages—it's the perfect crowd-pleaser.

MAKES 6 SERVINGS

2 pounds flank steak (or skirt steak)
Salt and pepper, to taste
1/2 cup chipotle salsa (see Terrific Tips)
1/2 cup cola
1/4 cup light brown sugar
1 teaspoon minced garlic
1 teaspoon dried oregano leaves
Warm flour tortillas, for serving
  (see Terrific Tips)
Onions, bell peppers, (see Terrific Tips)
  and shredded cheese, for serving
Condiments of your choice, for serving

Trim any excess fat from the flank steak. Season with salt and pepper. In a 2-quart glass oblong dish, mix together the chipotle salsa, cola, brown sugar, garlic, and oregano. Add the meat, cover with plastic wrap, and refrigerate for at least 1 hour or overnight.

When ready to serve, drain the meat well, and discard the marinade. Grill, broil, or pan sear over high heat, until the meat is cooked done, 5 to 8 minutes per side—flank steak should be served rare. Slice the meat thinly on an angle against the grain, and serve with the warm tortillas and accompaniments.

***Nutritional Information per Serving
(without tortillas or accompaniments)***
Calories 224, Protein (g) 29, Carbohydrate (g) 1, Fat (g) 11, Calories from Fat (%) 46, Saturated Fat (g) 5, Dietary Fiber (g) 0, Cholesterol (mg) 72, Sodium (mg) 357
Diabetic Exchanges: *4 lean meat*

Terrific Tips

▸ CHIPOTLE SALSA HAS A SMOKY, RICH FLAVOR, AND CAN BE FOUND IN THE SUPERMARKET IN THE SECTION WHERE THE SALSAS ARE SOLD.
▸ SLICE GREEN PEPPERS AND ONIONS, AND SAUTÉ THEM IN A SMALL AMOUNT OF OLIVE OIL OVER MEDIUM-HIGH HEAT UNTIL TENDER. SERVE WITH THE FAJITAS.
▸ TO WARM THE TORTILLAS, WRAP THEM IN FOIL AND HEAT IN A 350°F OVEN FOR 10 MINUTES.

Savory Southwestern Cheesecake

This crowd-pleasing recipe is great with tortilla chips and, best of all, you can make it ahead of time.

MAKES 20 TO 25 SERVINGS

2/3 cup finely crushed baked tortilla chips
2 tablespoons margarine, melted
2 (8-ounce) packages reduced-fat
  cream cheese, softened
2 eggs
1 cup shredded reduced-fat sharp
  Cheddar cheese
2 (4-ounce) cans chopped green chiles,
  drained
1 bunch green onions (scallions), chopped
1 teaspoon minced garlic
1 cup mild salsa

Preheat the oven to 350°F. Coat a 9-inch springform pan with nonstick cooking spray. In a mixing bowl, mix together the crushed tortilla chips and margarine, and press into the bottom of the prepared springform pan. Bake for 10 minutes, and set aside.

In a mixing bowl, mix together the cream cheese and eggs until creamy. Fold in the Cheddar cheese, green chiles, green onions, and garlic. Carefully spread half the mixture over the crust, top with the salsa, and cover with the remaining cheese mixture; do not mix. Bake for 30 to 40 minutes, or until the mixture is set. Remove from the oven, and let cool in the pan for 10 minutes. Run a knife around the inside edge to loosen, and remove the sides from the pan. Refrigerate until ready to serve.

Nutritional Information per Serving
Calories 84, Protein (g) 4, Carbohydrate (g) 3, Fat (g) 6, Calories from Fat (%) 67, Saturated Fat (g), 3, Dietary Fiber (g) 1, Cholesterol (mg) 32, Sodium (mg) 212
Diabetic Exchanges: *0.5 lean meat, 1 fat*

Terrific Tip

SOMETIMES I TOP THE SOUTHWESTERN CHEESECAKE WITH DIFFERENT FLAVORED SALSAS, AND WHEN I AM IN A CREATIVE MODE, I ADORN IT WITH SOUR CREAM, AND CHOPPED TOMATOES, ONIONS, AND OLIVES.

Yellow Rice with Black Beans and Roasted Peppers

*This vivid, colorful, full-flavored dish has such versatility. I wanted a rice dish
that I could serve for any occasion, Southwestern or otherwise, so I developed this recipe.
The bean and rice mixture may be mixed together and served as a room temperature salad.*

MAKES 6 TO 8 SERVINGS

2 (5-ounce) packages yellow rice
3 teaspoons ground cumin, divided
2 tablespoons lime juice
1 tablespoon olive oil
1 bunch green onions (scallions),
  sliced and divided
1 (15-ounce) can black beans, drained
  and rinsed
1/2 cup chopped jarred roasted red peppers
1/2 cup chopped green bell pepper
1/4 cup salsa

Prepare the rice according to the package directions.

In a small nonstick skillet over medium heat, stir 2 teaspoons of the cumin for about 1 minute. Remove from the heat, and stir in the lime juice and oil.

When the rice is done, add the remaining 1 teaspoon cumin, half of the green onions, and the heated cumin-lime juice mixture, and toss to combine. Arrange the rice mixture on a platter.

In a mixing bowl, mix together the remaining green onions, black beans, roasted red peppers, bell pepper, and salsa. Mound the bean mixture in the center of the rice, and serve.

Nutritional Information per Serving
*Calories 194, Protein (g) 6, Carbohydrate (g) 37, Fat (g) 2, Calories from Fat (%) 11,
Saturated Fat (g) 0, Dietary Fiber (g) 4, Cholesterol (mg) 0, Sodium (mg) 665*
Diabetic Exchanges: *0.5 very lean meat, 2.5 starch*

Creamy Pralines

Patience and a good candy thermometer are a must when making pralines, but they are worth the stirring.
Nuts contain the "good" fats so this isn't too bad of a splurge.

MAKES 36 SMALL PRALINES

3 cups light brown sugar
1 cup skim milk
1/4 teaspoon cream of tartar
1/8 teaspoon salt
11/2 cups coarsely chopped pecans
2 tablespoons margarine
1 teaspoon vanilla extract

In a large pot (the mixture will bubble up high), combine the sugar, milk, cream of tartar, and salt. Cook, stirring, over low heat until the sugar dissolves. Raise the heat to medium, and cook, stirring, until it reaches the soft ball stage, 236°F to 238°F on a candy thermometer. Remove from the heat, and cool the mixture to 220°F. Add the pecans, margarine, and vanilla, and stir only until the mixture is creamy, as it will harden quickly. Drop by spoonfuls on waxed paper.

Nutritional Information per Serving (per praline)
Calories 112, Protein (g) 1, Carbohydrate (g) 19, Fat (g) 4, Calories from Fat (%) 33,
Saturated Fat (g) 0, Dietary Fiber (g) 0, Cholesterol (mg) 0, Sodium (mg) 26
Diabetic Exchanges: *1.5 other carbohydrate, 1 fat*

Flan

This make-ahead custard dessert is the grand finale to a Mexican party.
It's easy to prepare, and guests will delight in every bite. Garnish with fresh berries.

MAKES 8 TO 10 SERVINGS

1/2 cup sugar
1 (12-ounce) can fat-free evaporated milk
1 (14-ounce) can fat-free sweetened
  condensed milk
3 eggs
2 egg whites
1 tablespoon vanilla extract

Preheat the oven to 325°F. Coat a 9-inch round cake pan with nonstick cooking spray.

Place the sugar in a heavy saucepan over medium heat, and cook, stirring frequently, until the sugar dissolves, about 5 minutes. Immediately pour into the prepared cake pan, tipping the pan quickly until the caramelized sugar coats the entire bottom of the pan.

In a food processor or mixer, mix together the evaporated milk, sweetened condensed milk, eggs, egg whites, and vanilla until blended. Pour into the cake pan. Place the cake pan in a 3-quart oblong baking dish, and add hot water to the dish to a depth of 1 inch. Carefully place in the oven, and bake for 1 hour, or until a knife inserted in the center comes out clean.

Remove the pan from the dish, and cool the pan completely on a wire rack. Cover, and refrigerate for at least 3 hours. Loosen the edge of the flan with a knife, and invert the flan onto a larger serving plate. Pour the remaining caramelized syrup over the flan.

Nutritional Information per Serving
Calories 210, Protein (g) 9, Carbohydrate (g) 39, Fat (g) 2, Calories from Fat (%) 7,
Saturated Fat (g) 1, Dietary Fiber (g) 0, Cholesterol (mg) 67, Sodium (mg) 115
Diabetic Exchanges: *1 skim milk, 1.5 other carbohydrate*

Terrific Tailgating

Living in Baton Rouge, the home of the Louisiana State University Tigers, I know first hand that tailgating is a very important fall social event. Whether you are attending a college football playoff or cheering on the pros, a scrumptious tailgating menu is an absolute must for any pre-game gathering. The food not only has to entice the taste buds of fans of all ages, it also needs to be grab-and-go and easy to serve. I always include hearty sandwiches for bigger appetites, a few inviting appetizers, a couple of tasty dips, and of course plenty of easy-to-eat and hard-to-resist brownies and cookies.

Select your menu according to your guests' tastes as well as the time and location of your party. Some of the best tailgating parties can take place in the comfort of your living room during the pre-game show! If you are gathering at the field or stadium, put your social graces aside and transport everything in disposable containers. Have an ice chest filled with ice packs to keep chilled items fresh, and always bring big garbage bags for quick-and-easy clean up. Then get ready to cheer—go Tigers!

MENU SELECTIONS

EXCITING EXTRAS

▶ Serve your dip in hollowed-out bread loaves for easy clean up and extra snacking (after all, the bowls are edible!).

▶ Hollow out large fruits such as pineapples or melons to form disposable bowls with pizzazz.

▶ Buy paper goods in your favorite team's colors and *really* show your spirit.

▶ Use colorful frilled toothpicks to skewer fruit for fruit kebobs. A little bit of frill goes a long way!

▶ Create a portable centerpiece by filling a basket with pots of daisies, a football, and pom-poms.

▶ Purchase a tube of icing, and decorate the top of each of the Chocolate Espresso Brownies

Short Cuts

▶ Order a fruit tray from the supermarket for serving with the Pineapple and Coconut Fruit Dip.

▶ Purchase brownies or cookies from your favorite local bakery. Dress them up with colorful frosting (in your team's colors) for a personal touch!

▶ Order some large sub sandwiches at the deli counter, and slice into small, individual pieces for easy eating.

Spinach Dip

Colorful dips look fabulous when served in hollowed-out bread loaves (see Terrific Tip, page 55). This spinach dip tastes great, and it's healthy too. The Italian dressing mix is the secret to this recipe—it adds ultimate flavor without the effort.

MAKES 24 (2-TABLESPOON) SERVINGS

1 (10-ounce) package frozen chopped
  spinach, thawed and squeezed dry
1 cup (8 ounces) fat-free sour cream
1/3 cup light mayonnaise
1 (0.7-ounce) package Italian dressing mix
1/2 cup sliced green onions (scallions)
1/2 cup chopped tomatoes
2 tablespoons lemon juice

In a large bowl, combine the spinach, sour cream, mayonnaise, Italian dressing mix, green onions, tomatoes, and lemon juice. Refrigerate until ready to serve. Serve with chips, veggies, or bread cubes.

Nutritional Information per Serving
Calories 30, Protein (g) 1, Carbohydrate (g) 4, Fat (g) 1, Calories from Fat (%) 36, Saturated Fat (g) 0, Dietary Fiber (g) 0, Cholesterol (mg) 3, Sodium (mg) 131
Diabetic Exchanges: *1 vegetable*

Artichoke Squares

This easy-to-prepare finger food will scores points with any crowd. The squares taste great whether served hot from the oven, at room temperature, or even cold. If you plan on traveling to the game, make this recipe ahead of time, refrigerate before cutting the squares (they are easier to cut when cold), and pile them on a tray to serve.

MAKES 30 TO 35 SQUARES

1 cup chopped onion
1 red bell pepper, cored and chopped
1 teaspoon minced garlic
2 (14-ounce) cans artichoke hearts, drained
  and chopped
2 eggs
2 egg whites
1 cup shredded reduced-fat sharp Cheddar
  cheese
1/3 cup Italian bread crumbs
1 teaspoon dried oregano leaves
Large dash hot sauce
Salt and pepper, to taste

Preheat the oven to 350°F.

Coat a medium skillet with nonstick cooking spray, and set over medium heat. Add the onion, red pepper, and garlic, and cook, stirring, until tender, about 5 minutes. Remove from the heat.

In a large bowl, add the sautéed vegetables, artichoke hearts, eggs, egg whites, cheese, bread crumbs, oregano, hot sauce, salt, and pepper, and stir to mix well. Coat a 2-quart oblong baking dish with nonstick cooking spray, and transfer the mixture to the prepared dish. Bake for 30 minutes, or until the mixture is set and light brown. Cut into squares for serving.

Nutritional Information per Serving (per square)
Calories 27, Protein (g) 2, Carbohydrate (g) 3, Fat (g) 1, Calories from Fat (%) 31, Saturated Fat (g) 0, Dietary Fiber (g) 0, Cholesterol (mg) 14, Sodium (mg) 81
Diabetic Exchanges: *1 vegetable*

Terrific Tip

SELECT AN UNCUT, ROUND, DARK BREAD AS A DISPOSABLE CONTAINER FOR DIP. SCOOP OUT THE SOFT CENTER OF THE BREAD, MAKING ROOM TO FILL WITH THE DIP. CUT THE EXTRA BREAD INTO CUBES OR CUBE AN ADDITIONAL LOAF OF BREAD TO SERVE WITH THE DIP.

PINEAPPLE AND COCONUT FRUIT DIP

Pineapple and Coconut Fruit Dip

This light and luscious dip works great with fruit kebobs. Choose your favorite seasonal fruits, from pineapple to berries, and skewer with colorful, frilled toothpicks.

MAKES 20 (2-TABLESPOON) SERVINGS

1 (8-ounce) can unsweetened crushed pineapple, undrained
3/4 cup skim milk
1 cup fat-free sour cream
1 (3.4-ounce) package instant coconut cream pudding mix

In a mixing bowl, mix together the pineapple and canning liquid, milk, sour cream, and coconut cream pudding mix. Refrigerate until well chilled.

Nutritional Information per Serving
Calories 43, Protein (g) 1, Carbohydrate (g) 8, Fat (g) 0, Calories from Fat (%) 0, Saturated Fat (g) 0, Dietary Fiber (g) 0, Cholesterol (mg) 2, Sodium (mg) 66
Diabetic Exchanges: *0.5 other carbohydrate*

Terrific Tip

MANY PEOPLE THINK THIS DIP IS SO GOOD YOU COULD EAT IT WITH A SPOON, SO HERE IS A DESSERT VARIATION: MAKE PARFAITS WITH THIS INCREDIBLE PUDDING DIP, LAYERED WITH WHIPPED TOPPING AND TOPPED WITH TOASTED COCONUT.

Marinated Artichoke Hearts

This simple recipe is as easy as opening a couple of cans, yet the result is amazing.
Using fresh rosemary makes a noticeable difference here, and you can use the extra sprigs as garnish.
Serve these tasty artichokes on frilled toothpicks, or coarsely chop them to top a sturdy cracker.

MAKES 10 TO 12 SERVINGS

2 tablespoons balsamic vinegar
2 tablespoons olive oil
1 teaspoon minced garlic
1½ teaspoons chopped fresh rosemary
 leaves, or ¾ teaspoon dried leaves
¼ teaspoon crushed red pepper flakes
2 (14-ounce) cans artichoke hearts,
 drained and quartered

In a small bowl, whisk together the balsamic vinegar, olive oil, garlic, rosemary, and red pepper flakes. Put the artichokes in a medium-size bowl, and pour the vinaigrette mixture over them. Refrigerate until serving. Serve chilled or at room temperature.

Nutritional Information per Serving
Calories 37, Protein (g) 1, Carbohydrate (g) 4, Fat (g) 2, Calories from Fat (%) 52,
Saturated Fat (g) 0, Dietary Fiber (g) 1, Cholesterol (mg) 0, Sodium (mg) 118
Diabetic Exchanges: *1 vegetable, 0.5 fat*

Tailgating Tortilla Bites

Simple to prepare and easy to eat, these pinwheels are packed with ham and the toasty crunch of pecans, and flavored with zesty Dijon mustard and dill. For added pizzazz, use different colored tortillas such as roasted red pepper and green spinach. Be sure to make plenty (doubling the recipe is easy to do) as they are the perfect pick-up snack, appealing to child and adult sports fans alike.

MAKES 36 TO 48 TORTILLA BITES, DEPENDING ON TORTILLA SIZE

1 (8-ounce) package reduced-fat cream
 cheese, softened
1 tablespoon Dijon mustard
1 teaspoon minced garlic
½ teaspoon dried dill weed leaves
6 ounces honey baked ham, cut into pieces
¼ cup chopped pecans, toasted
 (see Terrific Tip, page 22)
½ cup sliced green onions (scallions)
6 (6- to 8-inch) flour tortillas

In a mixing bowl, add the cream cheese, mustard, garlic, and dill weed, and stir to mix well. Add the ham, pecans, and green onions, mixing well. Divide and spread the filling to cover each tortilla and roll up tightly. Place the rolls seam-side down on a tray and refrigerate until well chilled. Cut each roll into 6 to 8 pinwheels, depending on the size of the tortillas.

Nutritional Information per Serving (per tortilla bite)
Calories 33, Protein (g) 2, Carbohydrate (g) 2, Fat (g) 2,
Calories from Fat (%) 51, Saturated Fat (g) 1, Dietary Fiber (g) 0,
Cholesterol (mg) 5, Sodium (mg) 87
Diabetic Exchanges: *0.5 fat*

Terrific Tip
THE FILLED TORTILLAS ARE MUCH EASIER TO CUT WHEN THE CREAM CHEESE FILLING HAS CHILLED. BE SURE TO PLAN AHEAD WHEN MAKING THIS DISH.

Marinated Pork Tenderloin with Honey Mustard Sauce

Slice the tenderloin, and serve it on a platter with the Honey Mustard Sauce in a small bowl and a basket of rolls or Yam Biscuits (recipe follows). Or you can prepare a tray of pork sandwiches in advance for easy-to-serve finger food.

MAKES 10 TO 12 SERVINGS

3 pounds pork tenderloin, trimmed of fat
2/3 cup reduced-sodium soy sauce
1/3 cup honey
1/4 cup firmly packed light brown sugar
1 tablespoon sesame oil
1 teaspoon minced garlic
1 teaspoon ground ginger
1/4 cup Honey Mustard Sauce
    (recipe follows), for serving

In a mixing bowl, add the soy sauce, honey, brown sugar, sesame oil, garlic, and ginger, and stir to mix well. Transfer the pork tenderloin to a zipper-top plastic bag along with the marinade mixture and seal. Marinate in the refrigerator all day or overnight. Cook on a medium-hot grill, or bake in a preheated 350°F oven for 45 minutes, until the internal temperature reaches 160°F. Cool, and cut into slices for serving. Serve with the Honey Mustard Sauce.

**Nutritional Information per Serving
(without Honey Mustard Sauce)**
*Calories 158, Protein (g) 25, Carbohydrate (g) 1, Fat (g) 5,
Calories from Fat (%) 30, Saturated Fat (g) 2, Dietary Fiber (g) 0,
Cholesterol (mg) 75, Sodium (mg) 399*
Diabetic Exchanges: *3 lean meat*

Terrific Tip
BE SURE TO BRING AN ICE CHEST WITH ICE PACKETS TO STORE ANY LEFTOVER FOOD UNTIL AFTER THE EVENT. INCLUDE EXTRA ZIPPER-TOP PLASTIC BAGS.

Honey Mustard Sauce

Sweet and spicy does the trick!

MAKES ABOUT 12 (1-TEASPOON) SERVINGS

3 tablespoons Dijon mustard
1 tablespoon honey
1/2 teaspoon horseradish sauce

In a small bowl, mix together the mustard, honey, and horseradish sauce. Serve alongside the Marinated Pork Tenderloin.

Nutritional Information per Serving
*Calories 10, Protein (g) 0, Carbohydrate (g) 2, Fat (g) 0, Calories from Fat (%) 0,
Saturated, Fat (g) 0, Dietary Fiber (g) 0, Cholesterol (mg) 0, Sodium (mg) 92*
Diabetic Exchanges: *Free*

Yam Biscuits

These yummy biscuits pair perfectly with the Marinated Pork Tenderloin (recipe above). Serve them right out of the oven, or let cool and use to create finger sandwiches. These biscuits make a nice addition to any brunch or lunch.

MAKES 18 BISCUITS

3 cups all-purpose baking mix
1 tablespoon sugar
1/2 teaspoon ground cinnamon
1/2 teaspoon ground nutmeg
1 (15-ounce) can sweet potatoes
    (yams), drained and mashed
3/4 cup skim milk

Preheat the oven to 450°F.
   In a large bowl, mix together the baking mix, sugar, cinnamon, and nutmeg. Add the sweet potatoes and milk, and mix until well combined.
   Roll out the mixture on a floured surface to 1 inch thick. Cut individual biscuits with a 2-inch cutter or an inverted glass, and place them on a baking sheet.
   Bake for 10 to 12 minutes, or until golden.

Nutritional Information per Serving (per biscuit)
*Calories 111, Protein (g) 2, Carbohydrate (g) 19, Fat (g) 3, Calories from Fat (%) 25,
Saturated Fat (g) 1, Dietary Fiber (g) 1, Cholesterol (mg) 0, Sodium (mg) 270*
Diabetic Exchanges: *1 starch, 0.5 fat*

CHOCOLATE ESPRESSO BROWNIES and COLORFUL BROWNIES

Chocolate Espresso Brownies

The espresso powder intensifies the rich chocolate flavor of these absolutely fabulous, cakelike brownies.
This recipe makes a ton, and I always have these ingredients on hand for an emergency pick-up dessert.
Top with some toasted nuts, if desired, or mix nuts into the icing for the deluxe version.

MAKES ABOUT 72 BROWNIES

1 cup water
1/3 cup canola oil
2 tablespoons instant espresso powder
2 cups all-purpose flour
13/4 cups sugar
1/3 cup cocoa
1/2 cup buttermilk
1 teaspoon baking soda
1 egg, beaten
Chocolate Espresso Icing (recipe follows)

CHOCOLATE ESPRESSO ICING:
6 tablespoons (3/4 stick) margarine
1/3 cup buttermilk
1/4 cup cocoa
1 tablespoon espresso powder
1 (16-ounce) box confectioners' sugar
1 teaspoon vanilla extract

Preheat the oven to 400°F. Coat a 15 x 10 x 1-inch baking pan with nonstick cooking spray.

In a small pot, combine the water and oil, and bring to a boil. Remove from the heat, and stir in the espresso powder until dissolved. In a large bowl, mix together the flour, sugar, and cocoa. Add the hot water mixture to the flour mixture, and stir well. In a small bowl, mix together the buttermilk and baking soda, stirring until the baking soda dissolves. Add the buttermilk mixture and egg to the batter, stirring well.

Transfer the batter to the prepared baking pan. Bake for 15 minutes, or just until the top springs back when touched. Remove from the oven, immediately pour the Chocolate Espresso Icing on top, and spread. Cool the brownies completely at room temperature, and cut into squares.

Chocolate Espresso Icing: In a medium pot, combine the margarine, buttermilk, cocoa, and espresso powder, and bring to a boil. Add the confectioners' sugar and vanilla, mixing until smooth. Set aside until ready to use.

Nutritional Information per Serving (per brownie)
Calories 79, Protein (g) 1, Carbohydrate (g) 14, Fat (g) 2, Calories from Fat (%) 25,
Saturated Fat (g) 0, Dietary Fiber (g) 0, Cholesterol (mg) 3, Sodium (mg) 33
Diabetic Exchanges: *1.5 other carbohydrate, 1 fat*

Colorful Brownies

Tailgaters of all ages will grab these blonde, candy-filled brownies. For various holidays, purchase the milk chocolate candies coated in seasonal colors for a special festive touch.

MAKES 36 BROWNIES

½ cup (1 stick) margarine, melted
2 cups light brown sugar
2 eggs
1 teaspoon vanilla extract
1½ cups all-purpose flour
1 teaspoon baking powder
1 cup candy coated milk chocolate candies

Preheat the oven to 350°F. Coat a 13 x 9 x 2-inch baking pan with nonstick cooking spray.

In a large bowl, mix together the margarine and brown sugar. Add the eggs and vanilla, beating well.

In a separate bowl, mix together the flour and baking powder. Add the flour mixture to the margarine-sugar mixture, and stir just until combined. Stir in the chocolate candies.

Transfer the batter to the prepared pan, and bake for 25 to 30 minutes, or until an inserted toothpick comes out clean. Avoid overbaking, as the brownies harden as they cool. Cool in the pan on a wire rack, cut into squares, and serve.

Nutritional Information per Serving (per brownie)
*Calories 120, Protein (g) 1, Carbohydrate (g) 20, Fat (g) 4, Calories from Fat (%) 30,
Saturated Fat (g) 1, Dietary Fiber (g) 0, Cholesterol (mg) 13, Sodium (mg) 55*
Diabetic Exchanges: *1.5 other carbohydrate, 1 fat*

White Chocolate and Apricot Oatmeal Cookies

Oatmeal cookies are one of my favorite treats! Wait until you try this incredible, light variation on the traditional recipe, incorporating the sweetness of white chocolate and tartness of apricots.

MAKES 48 COOKIES

½ cup (1 stick) margarine, softened
½ cup sugar
½ cup light brown sugar
1 egg
1 cup all-purpose flour
1 teaspoon baking soda
2 cups oatmeal
⅔ cup white chocolate chips
1 cup chopped dried apricots

Preheat the oven to 375°F. Coat a baking sheet with nonstick cooking spray.

In a mixing bowl, beat the margarine, sugar, and brown sugar, until fluffy. Add the egg and beat well.

In a separate bowl, mix together the flour and baking soda. Gradually add the flour to the margarine-sugar mixture, and mix just until combined. Stir in the oatmeal, white chocolate chips, and apricots.

Drop the dough by teaspoons onto the prepared baking sheet. Bake for 8 to 10 minutes, or until the cookies are lightly browned on the bottom. Transfer to a sheet of waxed paper to cool to room temperature before serving.

Nutritional Information per Serving (per cookie)
*Calories 84, Protein (g) 1, Carbohydrate (g) 13, Fat (g) 3, Calories from Fat (%) 36,
Saturated Fat (g) 1, Dietary Fiber (g) 1, Cholesterol (mg) 5, Sodium (mg) 54*
Diabetic Exchanges: *1 other carbohydrate, 0.5 fat*

Backyard Barbecue

Whether you're celebrating Memorial Day, the Fourth of July, or Labor Day, or just enjoying a warm summer afternoon, there's always a reason to barbecue. Some people like using charcoal to cook the old-fashioned way, while others prefer to use gas for a less messy option. I sometimes cheat and prepare my smoky rich barbecue in the oven, the secret to obtaining that authentic barbecue flavor being the sauce. Just wait until you try my Pulled Barbecue Pork!

While everyone has their own barbecue style, the meal is never complete without summer sides like coleslaw and potato salad. And make sure to save room for dessert! My fun, eye-catching Burger Cake is fabulous, and nothing beats the incredible Apple Cobbler. A barbecue spread guarantees good food and a good time, and it's an ideal way to entertain company or host a family gathering.

MENU SELECTIONS

EXCITING EXTRAS

▶ Use bandanas or napkins as accent pieces to line a basket of muffins or tie to serving pieces.

▶ Wrap silverware in paper bandana napkins and tie with raffia (thin rope twine).

▶ Try the Burger Cake when you're short on time but still want to impress your guests—it's an easy recipe that makes a statement.

▶ If you have an ice cream machine, make homemade vanilla ice cream to serve with cobbler.

▶ Simple, inexpensive flowers (like mums) placed in a casual container add plenty of color to a backyard party.

Short Cuts

▶ Make the Pulled Barbecue Pork ahead of time, and reheat with the sauce.

▶ Make only one salad yourself, and purchase another one already made.

▶ Pick up rolls instead of baking cornbread muffins.

▶ Boil frozen corn-on-the-cob pieces inside and serve in a big bowl.

▶ Order brisket and chicken from your favorite barbecue restaurant to make sides.

In my cookbooks, there always has to be a recipe for a Spinach Artichoke Dip. Here's a quick recipe that will satisfy all those who know and love this popular dip. My daughters prepare this easy recipe as a snack. Serve with crackers.

MAKES 48 (2-TABLESPOON) SERVINGS

3 (10-ounce) packages frozen chopped spinach

1/2 cup chopped onion

1 teaspoon minced garlic

1 (8-ounce) package reduced-fat cream cheese

1 tablespoon Worcestershire sauce

Dash hot sauce

1 (5-ounce) can fat-free evaporated milk

1 cup shredded reduced-fat Swiss cheese

1/4 cup grated Parmesan cheese

1 (14-ounce) can artichoke hearts, drained and chopped

Salt and pepper, to taste

Cook the spinach according to the package directions, and drain well.

Coat a large pot with nonstick cooking spray, and set over medium heat. Add the onion and garlic, and cook, stirring, until tender, 3 to 5 minutes. Add the cream cheese, stirring until creamy. Add the spinach, Worcestershire sauce, and hot sauce, and gradually stir in evaporated milk, mixing well. Add the Swiss cheese and Parmesan cheese, stirring until the cheese is melted. Add the artichoke, stir, and season to taste with salt and pepper. Serve warm.

Nutritional Information per Serving
Calories 30, Protein (g) 2, Carbohydrate (g) 2, Fat (g) 2, Calories from Fat (%) 48, Saturated Fat (g) 1, Dietary Fiber (g) 1, Cholesterol (mg) 5, Sodium (mg) 78
Diabetic Exchanges: *0.5 fat*

The versatility of this dip is amazing. Served warm with crackers or crostini bread, it's rich with flavors that work perfectly together. It's just as good served cold with veggies, or try using it as a filling for hollowed-out cherry tomatoes. Whichever way you serve this dip, it is a blue cheese palate pleaser.

MAKES 16 (2-TABLESPOON) SERVINGS

1 (8-ounce) package reduced-fat cream cheese

4 ounces blue cheese

1/4 cup fat-free evaporated milk

2 slices center cut bacon, crisply cooked and crumbled

2 tablespoons chopped green onion (scallion) stems

In a microwaveable dish, combine the cream cheese, blue cheese, and evaporated milk. Cook for 1 minute, stir, and then cook for 1 minute longer, or until the cheese is melted. Add the bacon and green onion. Serve warm.

Nutritional Information per Serving
Calories 67, Protein (g) 4, Carbohydrate (g) 1, Fat (g) 5, Calories from Fat (%) 73, Saturated Fat (g) 3, Dietary Fiber (g) 0, Cholesterol (mg) 16, Sodium (mg) 180
Diabetic Exchanges: *0.5 very lean meat, 1 fat*

TEX-MEX CORN ON THE COB

Tex-Mex Corn on the Cob

Here's a recipe that spices up fresh corn while adding color to your platter.
With so much flavor, it's ready to eat without extra condiments.

MAKES 6 SERVINGS

3 tablespoons margarine, melted
1/2 teaspoon chili powder
1/2 teaspoon ground cumin
1/4 teaspoon dried oregano leaves
1/4 teaspoon garlic salt
Salt and pepper, to taste
6 ears cooked fresh corn

In a small bowl, mix together the margarine, chili powder, cumin, oregano, garlic, salt, and pepper. Drizzle over a platter of cooked fresh corn.

Nutritional Information per Serving
Calories 130, Protein (g) 3, Carbohydrate (g) 17, Fat (g) 7, Calories from Fat (%) 43,
Saturated Fat (g) 1, Dietary Fiber (g) 3, Cholesterol (mg) 0, Sodium (mg) 122
Diabetic Exchanges: *1 starch, 1 fat*

Pulled Barbecue Pork

*This specially seasoned shredded pork is referred to as "pulled pork." I serve it with the perfectly balanced Barbecue Sauce,
and it's definitely a family favorite. Leftovers are great on just a bun as the pork is the star of this show.*

MAKES 10 TO 12 SERVINGS

1 (4-pound) boneless pork sirloin roast,
   trimmed of excess fat
4 cloves garlic
2 tablespoons dark brown sugar
2 teaspoons dried thyme leaves
1/2 teaspoon cayenne pepper
1 teaspoon black pepper
Salt, to taste
Barbecue Sauce (recipe follows)

BARBECUE SAUCE:
1/2 cup chopped onion
1 (15-ounce) can tomato sauce
1 (12-ounce) bottle chili sauce
1/3 cup dark brown sugar
3 tablespoons cider vinegar
2 teaspoons ground thyme
1 1/2 teaspoons ground dry mustard
1 teaspoon ground allspice
Salt and pepper, to taste

Preheat the oven to 325°F. Make slits in the roast. Cut the garlic into slivers, and stuff into the slits in the roast.

In a small bowl, mix together the brown sugar, thyme, cayenne pepper, black pepper, and salt. Pat the sugar mixture all over the roast, place in a roasting pan, cover, and bake for 3 hours, or until the pork is very tender and the internal temperature reaches 160°F. (You may also cook the pork in a smoker.)

Using two forks, pull the pork apart into shreds. Spoon the desired amount of Barbecue Sauce over the meat, and toss to combine. Serve with extra Barbecue Sauce.

Barbecue Sauce: Coat a medium pot with nonstick cooking spray, and set over medium heat. Add the onion, and cook, stirring, until tender, 3 to 5 minutes. Add the tomato sauce, chili sauce, brown sugar, vinegar, thyme, dry mustard, allspice, salt, and pepper. Bring to a boil, reduce the heat, and simmer for 10 to 15 minutes to thicken. Remove from the heat, and serve.

Nutritional Information per Serving
*Calories 286, Protein (g) 31, Carbohydrate (g) 19, Fat (g) 9, Calories from Fat (%) 29,
Saturated Fat (g) 3, Dietary Fiber (g) 1, Cholesterol (mg) 91, Sodium (mg) 644*
Diabetic Exchanges: *4 lean meat, 1 other carbohydrate*

Glazed Barbecue Chicken

*Update your barbecue chicken with this new version featuring the exciting, bold flavor of hoisin sauce,
available in the Chinese section at most supermarkets. The sauce is what makes this a fantastic and memorable chicken dish.
Grilling is great, but this recipe is also fabulous when broiled or baked in the oven.*

MAKES 6 SERVINGS

1/2 cup bottled chili sauce
1/2 cup hoisin sauce
2 tablespoons honey
4 teaspoons Dijon mustard
1 teaspoon minced garlic
1/2 teaspoon crushed red pepper flakes
Salt and pepper, to taste
6 large chicken breasts (not boneless,
   2 1/4 pounds), skin removed

In a large mixing bowl or baking dish, mix together the chili sauce, hoisin sauce, honey, mustard, garlic, and red pepper flakes. Season the chicken breasts with salt and pepper, then add the chicken to the mixing bowl and coat with the sauce. Cover the chicken and let marinate in the refrigerator until ready to cook, up to overnight.

When ready to serve, either prepare a medium-hot grill or preheat the broiler. Grill the chicken until done, about 15 minutes on each side, or broil until done, 15 to 20 minutes on each side.

Nutritional Information per Serving
*Calories 205, Protein (g) 39, Carbohydrate (g) 5, Fat (g) 2, Calories from Fat (%) 10,
Saturated Fat (g) 1, Dietary Fiber (g) 0, Cholesterol (mg) 99, Sodium (mg) 357*
Diabetic Exchanges: *5 very lean meat, 0.5 other carbohydrate*

Roasted Potato Salad

You'll love this salad made with nicely roasted potatoes, rich with flavor, and tossed with fresh parsley and onions in a light dressing.

MAKES 8 SERVINGS

3 red potatoes, cut in large chunks
2 tablespoons olive oil
1 tablespoon Dijon mustard
6 cloves garlic, cut in large slivers
Salt and pepper, to taste
1/3 cup chopped fresh parsley
1/2 cup thinly sliced green onions (scallions)
1/2 cup nonfat plain yogurt

Preheat the oven to 400°F. Coat a baking sheet with nonstick cooking spray.

In a mixing bowl, combine the potato chunks, olive oil, mustard, garlic, salt, and pepper, tossing to coat. Place the potato chunks on the prepared baking sheet. Bake, stirring occasionally, for 30 minutes, or until tender.

Cool the potatoes to room temperature. Transfer to a mixing bowl, and toss with the parsley and green onions. Season with salt and pepper, and toss with the yogurt. Serve at room temperature or chilled.

Nutritional Information per Serving
Calories 85, Protein (g) 3, Carbohydrate (g) 12, Fat (g) 3, Calories from Fat (%) 34, Saturated Fat (g) 0, Dietary Fiber (g) 2, Cholesterol (mg) 0, Sodium (mg) 60
Diabetic Exchanges: *1 starch, 0.5 fat*

Pasta Coleslaw

*Pasta and coleslaw team up to create a trendy salad with a fabulous, light-and-creamy dressing.
Purchase a bag of shredded cabbage and the hard part is done.*

MAKES 6 TO 8 SERVINGS

8 ounces fussilli or farfalle pasta
2 cups shredded purple cabbage
1 cup chopped tomato
1 cup chopped green bell pepper
1/2 cup chopped green onions (scallions)
1 1/2 cups Creamy Dressing (recipe follows)

CREAMY DRESSING:
1/3 cup nonfat plain yogurt
1/4 cup light mayonnaise
1 tablespoon lemon juice
1/2 teaspoon minced garlic
1/2 teaspoon dried tarragon leaves
Salt and pepper, to taste

Cook the pasta according to the package instructions, drain, and set aside. In a large mixing bowl, mix together the cooked pasta, cabbage, tomato, bell pepper, and green onions. Toss with the Creamy Dressing, and refrigerate until ready to serve.

Creamy Dressing: In a small mixing bowl, mix together the yogurt, mayonnaise, lemon juice, garlic, tarragon, salt, and pepper.

Nutritional Information per Serving
Calories 154, Protein (g) 5, Carbohydrate (g) 26, Fat (g) 3, Calories from Fat (%) 18, Saturated Fat (g) 1, Dietary Fiber (g) 2, Cholesterol (mg) 3, Sodium (mg) 74
Diabetic Exchanges: *1.5 starch, 1 vegetable, 0.5 fat*

Mini Surprise Corn Muffins

When I tested this recipe, I made the cornbread from scratch. Then, I tried another version with the box mix that was even better and quicker. The hint of salsa with the green chiles and green onions compliments the traditional cornbread flavor. I like to serve these muffins in a basket.

MAKES ABOUT 30 MINIATURE MUFFINS

2 (8-ounce) packages corn muffin mix
2/3 cup shredded reduced-fat sharp
  Cheddar cheese
2/3 cup skim milk
1/2 cup sliced green onions (scallions)
1 (4-ounce) can green chiles, drained
2 eggs
1 cup salsa

Terrific Tip

USE THIS CORN MUFFIN RECIPE TO MAKE REGULAR SIZED MUFFINS. THE MUFFINS WILL NEED TO BAKE FOR A LITTLE LONGER, AND THE RECIPE WILL YIELD ONLY ABOUT 12 MUFFINS.

Preheat the oven to 400°F. Line miniature muffin tins with papers or coat with nonstick cooking spray.

In a large bowl, combine the corn muffin mix, cheese, milk, green onions, green chiles, and eggs, stirring until moistened. Spoon a little batter mixture into each tin, top each with about a teaspoon of salsa, and cover with more batter, filling the tins about two-thirds full. Bake for 10 to 12 minutes, or until the muffins are golden and spring back when touched.

Nutritional Information per Serving (per muffin)
*Calories 81, Protein (g) 2, Carbohydrate (g) 11, Fat (g) 3, Calories from Fat (%) 30,
Saturated Fat (g) 1, Dietary Fiber (g) 1, Cholesterol (mg) 16, Sodium (mg) 243*
Diabetic Exchanges: *1 starch, 0.5 fat*

Apple Cobbler

I usually like to prepare my fruit desserts with a crumbly topping, but I wanted to try something different this time, covering the out-of-this-world apple filling with a biscuit topping. Of course, the ultimate way to serve this treat is heated with a scoop of low-fat vanilla ice cream.

MAKES 8 SERVINGS

7 to 8 tart baking apples, peeled, pared,
  and sliced (about 10 cups)
1/4 cup maple syrup
1/4 cup light brown sugar
2 tablespoons all-purpose flour
1 tablespoon lemon juice
1/2 teaspoon ground cinnamon
1/4 teaspoon ground nutmeg
Topping (recipe follows)
Cinnamon and sugar

TOPPING:
1 1/3 cups all-purpose flour
1/3 cup plus 2 tablespoons skim milk
5 tablespoons margarine, softened
2 tablespoons sugar
2 teaspoons baking powder

Preheat the oven to 375°F. Coat a 13 x 9 x 2-inch baking dish with nonstick cooking spray.

In a large mixing bowl, combine the sliced apples, maple syrup, brown sugar, flour, lemon juice, cinnamon, and nutmeg, toss to coat the apples well, and transfer to the prepared baking dish. Cover with the Topping. Sprinkle the top with cinnamon and sugar. Bake for 40 to 45 minutes, or until the apples are tender and the Topping is golden brown.

Topping: In a mixing bowl, combine the flour, milk, margarine, sugar, and baking powder, mixing with a fork until blended. Pat onto a floured surface with your hand or a rolling pin until 1/4 inch thick. Cut into strips, triangles, or various shapes and place on top of the apple mixture.

Nutritional Information per Serving
*Calories 281, Protein (g) 3, Carbohydrate (g) 52, Fat (g) 8, Calories from Fat (%) 24,
Saturated Fat (g) 1, Dietary Fiber (g) 3, Cholesterol (mg) 0, Sodium (mg) 216*
Diabetic Exchanges: *1 starch, 1 fruit, 1.5 other carbohydrate, 1.5 fat*

Burger Cake

This cake will be the talk of the party! The yellow cake layer represents the bun, the brownie layer serves as the hamburger, and the yellow whipped topping makes a great mustard. Kiwi becomes lettuce and pickles, while strawberries stand in for tomatoes. You'll be using easy cake mixes, so don't let the length of this recipe intimidate you.

MAKES 20 SERVINGS

YELLOW CAKE LAYER:
1 (18.25-ounce) package yellow cake mix
3 egg whites
1 egg
2 tablespoons canola oil
1 1/3 cups water

1 cup confectioners' sugar
2 to 3 tablespoons skim milk
1 (9-inch-round) Brownie Layer (recipe follows)
1 envelope whipped topping mix
1/2 cup cold milk
1 teaspoon yellow food coloring
1 1/2 cups sliced strawberries
4 kiwis, peeled and thinly sliced
1/4 teaspoon poppy seeds

BROWNIE LAYER:
1 (18.25-ounce) package brownie mix
1/3 cup canola oil
1/4 cup water
2 eggs

Terrific Tip
MAKE CUPCAKES WITH THE EXTRA BATTER FROM THE YELLOW CAKE, SINCE YOU ONLY NEED ONE LAYER.

Prepare the Yellow Cake Layer: Preheat the oven to 350°F. Coat a 9-inch round cake pan with nonstick cooking spray.

In a large mixing bowl, beat together the cake mix, egg whites, egg, oil, and water until well mixed. Pour half the batter into the prepared pan. (You'll need only one yellow layer for this recipe—save the remaining batter for another use.) Bake for 25 to 30 minutes, or until the top springs back when touched. Cool the layer in the pan on a wire rack for 10 minutes, then turn out the cake onto the wire rack to cool.

To assemble, when the cake has cooled, split the layer in half into two 9-inch rounds with a long, serrated knife. Place the bottom half on serving plate. In a small bowl, mix together the confectioners' sugar and enough skim milk to form a spreadable consistency. Spread half of the mixture on top of the bottom yellow cake layer. Top with the cooled Brownie Layer.

In a mixing bowl, beat together the whipped topping mix, cold milk, and yellow food coloring until the topping is very thick and forms a peak. Spread the remaining half of the confectioners' sugar mixture on top of the brownie layer to help the next layer of fruit stay in place. Cover with sliced strawberries and kiwis. Top with the whipped topping mixture, making sure that the fruit is showing on all sides. Carefully place the remaining half of the yellow cake layer on top of the fruit and whipped topping. Sprinkle the top with poppy seeds, and refrigerate until ready to serve.

Brownie Layer: Preheat the oven to 350°F. Coat a 9-inch round cake pan with nonstick cooking spray.

In a large mixing bowl, beat together the brownie mix, oil, water, and eggs until well mixed. Pour the batter into the prepared pan, and bake for 20 to 25 minutes, or until the top springs back when touched. Cool in the pan for 10 minutes, then turn out onto a wire rack to cool completely before using.

Nutritional Information per Serving
Calories 265, Protein (g) 3, Carbohydrate (g) 42, Fat (g) 10, Calories from Fat (%) 32, Saturated Fat (g) 2, Dietary Fiber (g) 1, Cholesterol (mg) 30, Sodium (mg) 288
Diabetic Exchanges: *3 other carbohydrate, 2 fat*

BURGER CAKE

Glitz & Glitter Dessert Party

Glitz and glitter is the best way to describe my elegant yet easy dessert party. This fabulous affair is always full of perks (and I'm not just talking about the coffee!) as everyone feels free to indulge in luscious desserts that they may have otherwise avoided. An abundance of gold decorations and candles sets the mood, and once the desserts are out, you'll find yourself free from most hosting duties and able to relax and truly enjoy your company.

You can offer a variety of desserts in individual servings or larger, elegant presentations. You may find that any one dessert serves more people than normal—everyone wants to taste each treat, and they will often try only a small portion before moving on to the next. Estimate the number of people coming to determine how many different desserts to prepare. There have been times when I have served just two different trifles, while other successful parties required a larger assortment of recipes.

For this type of party, you only need forks and plates. I often use my china for an extra touch of refinement, but small, clear plastic plates provide a classy yet disposable alternative. However, I always insist upon using real silverware.

When serving coffee, try offering one or two flavored coffees and always have a pot of decaffeinated available. I also like to have an assortment of liqueurs on a tray beside the coffee for those adults who desire that added kick. If serving champagne, set empty glasses on a tray with a champagne bucket, enabling guests to serve themselves.

So when is the best time for dessert entertaining? I love to throw a Glitz and Glitter party during the busy holiday season, when guests often need to come and go quickly or are just dropping by on their way to another soiree. Dessert parties also work well when gathering after a play, symphony, or a similar social event.

MENU SELECTIONS

EXCITING EXTRAS

- Serve a variety of flavored coffees.
- Use a deviled egg dish to serve the coffee condiments.
- Float raspberries in the champagne.
- Prepare the Bundt cake in a fancy mold.
- Use small china plates and linen cocktail napkins for extra elegance.
- Serve the Tiramisu in champagne glasses or goblets.
- Remember, candles are just as effective as flowers at enhancing the atmosphere of your party. Arrange lighted candles around your table.

Short Cuts

- Serve the Tiramisu in a trifle dish or a large glass bowl instead of individual serving dishes.
- Use small, clear plastic plates for easy clean-up.
- Supplement your dessert menu by making a trip to your favorite bakery— don't tell!
- Use attractive, more formal paper cocktail napkins.
- Serve only pick-up desserts (like cookies and brownies) that don't require silver-ware for eating.

Banana Éclair

This impressive "show stopper" tastes even better than it looks. Anytime we have guests, my husband immediately requests that I include this dessert on the menu. It's gorgeous and absolutely delicious. To prepare in advance, make the éclair shell ahead of time. To serve, slice the éclair in half lengthwise, then cut in slices down the middle—you will be able to serve quite a crowd.

MAKES 16 TO 18 SERVINGS

1 cup water
½ cup (1 stick) margarine
1 cup all-purpose flour
2 tablespoons sugar
2 eggs
3 egg whites
Banana Cream Filling (recipe follows)
2 to 3 bananas, sliced
Chocolate Glaze (recipe follows)
¼ cup coarsely chopped walnuts, toasted
 (see Terrific Tip, page 22)
Fresh strawberries, for garnish

BANANA CREAM FILLING:
2 envelopes whipped topping mix
1 cup cold skim milk
2 cups mashed bananas (4 to 5)
¼ cup crème de cocoa (optional)
1 teaspoon vanilla extract

CHOCOLATE GLAZE:
2 tablespoons cocoa
¼ teaspoon vanilla extract
⅔ cup confectioners' sugar
2 tablespoons hot water

Preheat the oven to 400°F. Coat a 10 x 15 x 1-inch jelly-roll pan with nonstick cooking spray.

In a large saucepan, bring the water and margarine to a boil over medium heat, cooking until the margarine is melted. In a small bowl, combine the flour with the sugar, and add all at once to the saucepan, stirring vigorously with a spoon until the dough forms a ball and leaves the sides of the pan. Remove the pan from the heat. Beat in the eggs and egg whites with a spoon, one at a time, and continue beating until the dough is stiff and glossy.

On the prepared jelly-roll pan, form about two-thirds of the dough into one long oblong about 7 inches wide. Spoon the remaining third of the dough into mounds along the top of the oblong. Bake for 20 to 25 minutes, or until golden brown. Remove from the oven, and, with a sharp knife, make slits along the sides of the éclair about 2 inches apart to let the steam escape. Return to the oven, and continue baking for 10 minutes longer. Remove the pan to a cooling rack.

Carefully slice off the top of the éclair—it may come off in pieces. Remove the top, and scoop out any soft dough inside the shell. Cool thoroughly. Place the éclair bottom on a serving platter, and fill with half the Banana Cream Filling. Add a layer of sliced bananas, and then cover with the remaining Filling. Cover with pieces of the top shell to form the top of éclair, if not in one whole piece. Drizzle with the Chocolate Glaze. Sprinkle with the toasted walnuts. Refrigerate until serving time. Before serving, garnish the éclair with fresh strawberries.

Banana Cream Filling: In a large mixing bowl, combine both envelopes of the whipped topping and the milk, beating until the topping is very thick and forms a peak. In another mixing bowl, mix together the mashed bananas, crème de cocoa, and vanilla. With a rubber spatula, fold the banana mixture into the whipped topping.

Chocolate Glaze: In a small bowl, mix together the cocoa, vanilla, and confectioners' sugar. Stir in the hot water to make a thin glaze. Set aside until ready to use.

Nutritional Information per Serving
Calories 192, Protein (g) 3, Carbohydrate (g) 26, Fat (g) 8, Calories from Fat (%) 37, Saturated Fat (g) 2, Dietary Fiber (g) 1, Cholesterol (mg) 24, Sodium (mg) 89
Diabetic Exchanges: *1.5 other carbohydrate, 1.5 fat*

Terrific Tip

WHEN REMOVING THE TOP OF THE ÉCLAIR, DON'T FRET IF IT BREAKS INTO PIECES—YOU WON'T BE ABLE TO TELL ONCE THE RECIPE IS ASSEMBLED. EVEN IF THE BOTTOM HAS HOLES, IT WILL BE FINE AS IT ONLY SERVES AS A BASE TO HOLD THE FILLING. AFTER FILLING, JUST LAY THE PIECES TO FORM THE TOP OVER THE FILLING, AND DRIZZLE WITH CHOCOLATE SAUCE. WHEN I MADE THIS RECIPE TO BE PHOTOGRAPHED FOR THIS BOOK, MY ÉCLAIR TOP WAS IN MANY PIECES, BUT YOU WOULD NEVER KNOW (SHHH!).

BANANA ÉCLAIR

Baked Pears with Orange Marmalade Sauce

Don't let the chore of coring pears intimidate you—this dessert may be made in the morning, when you perhaps have a bit more time, and reheated when ready to serve. It also makes an impressive individual dessert for a dinner party.

MAKES 4 SERVINGS

1 cup water

1 cup orange juice

1 tablespoon orange liqueur (optional)

4 pears, peeled and cored, leaving
  stems attached

3/4 cup orange marmalade

1 tablespoon light brown sugar

1 tablespoon margarine

1/4 teaspoon ground cinnamon

1/4 cup sliced almonds, toasted
  (see Terrific Tip, page 22)

In a large pot, combine the water, orange juice, and orange liqueur, and bring to a boil. Place the pears in the boiling mixture, return to a boil, reduce the heat, cover, and simmer for about 15 minutes, or until the pears are tender. With a slotted spoon, carefully remove the pears to a platter, reserving 2 tablespoons of the cooking liquid.

For the sauce, in a small pot, combine the marmalade, brown sugar, margarine, cinnamon, and reserved pear cooking liquid. Bring to a boil for 1 minute. Serve the pears with the warm sauce, and sprinkle with the almonds.

Nutritional Information per Serving
Calories 344, Protein (g) 2, Carbohydrate (g) 74, Fat (g) 7, Calories from Fat (%) 16, Saturated Fat (g) 1, Dietary Fiber (g) 4, Cholesterol (mg) 0, Sodium (mg) 69
Diabetic Exchanges: *2 fruit, 3 other carbohydrate, 1.5 fat*

CHOCOLATE ITALIAN
CREAM CAKE

Chocolate Italian Cream Cake

My lightened Italian Cream Cake was the #1 recipe in Cooking Light Magazine's tenth-anniversary issue and was featured on the cover. Here is a chocolate version of what I consider to be my all-time personal favorite—it's truly the best cake ever!

MAKES 16 TO 20 SERVINGS

½ cup (1 stick) margarine, softened

¼ cup canola oil

2 cups sugar

2 eggs, separated

2 cups all-purpose flour

¼ cup cocoa

1 teaspoon baking soda

1 cup buttermilk

1 tablespoon vanilla extract

1 teaspoon coconut extract

½ cup chopped pecans

½ cup flaked coconut

4 egg whites

Chocolate Cream Cheese Icing
  (recipe follows)

CHOCOLATE CREAM CHEESE ICING:

1 (8-ounce) package reduced-fat cream
  cheese, softened

3 tablespoons margarine, softened

1 (16-ounce) box confectioners' sugar

¼ cup cocoa

1 teaspoon vanilla extract

Preheat the oven to 350°F. Coat 3 (9-inch) round cake pans with nonstick cooking spray.

In a mixing bowl, beat the margarine and oil until creamy. Gradually add the sugar, beating until light and fluffy. Add the 2 egg yolks, one at a time, beating well after each addition. In a separate mixing bowl, mix together the flour, cocoa, and baking soda. Add the flour mixture to the sugar mixture, alternating with the buttermilk and ending with the flour, beating after each addition. Add the vanilla, coconut extract, pecans, and coconut, and mix well.

In a separate mixing bowl, beat all 6 egg whites until stiff peaks form (see Terrific Tip). With a rubber spatula, fold the beaten egg whites into the batter mixture. Pour the batter evenly into the prepared cake pans. Bake for 20 to 25 minutes, until the tops spring back when touched. Cool the cakes in the pans for 10 minutes, then turn them out onto racks to cool thoroughly. Frost the layers and sides with Chocolate Cream Cheese Icing.

Chocolate Cream Cheese Icing: In a mixing bowl, beat the cream cheese and margarine until smooth. In a small bowl, mix together a few tablespoons of the confectioners' sugar with the cocoa, and add to the cream cheese mixture. Gradually add the remaining confectioners' sugar, beating until light. Blend in the vanilla.

Nutritional Information per Serving
Calories 382, Protein (g) 5, Carbohydrate (g) 56, Fat (g) 16, Calories from Fat (%) 36, Saturated Fat (g) 4, Dietary Fiber (g) 1, Cholesterol (mg) 30, Sodium (mg) 225
Diabetic Exchanges: *3.5 other carbohydrate, 3 fat*

Almond Chocolate Sandies

You will find yourself reaching over and over again for these melt-in-your-mouth cookies,
filled with crunchy toasted almonds and semisweet chocolate.

MAKES 30 COOKIES

½ cup (1 stick) margarine, softened
2 tablespoons sugar
1 tablespoon light brown sugar
1 teaspoon almond extract
1 cup all-purpose flour
½ cup semisweet chocolate chips
⅓ cup chopped slivered almonds, toasted
 (see Terrific Tip, page 22)
½ cup confectioners' sugar

Preheat the oven to 350°F.

In a mixing bowl, beat together the margarine, sugar, brown sugar, and almond extract. Gradually add the flour, mixing just until blended. Stir in the chocolate chips and almonds. Roll the dough into small balls and bake on an ungreased baking sheet for 15 minutes, or until lightly golden brown. Roll the cookies in the confectioners' sugar while still warm. Cool at room temperature before serving.

Nutritional Information per Serving (per cookie)
Calories 77, Protein (g) 1, Carbohydrate (g) 9, Fat (g) 5, Calories from Fat (%) 51, Saturated Fat (g) 1, Dietary Fiber (g) 0, Cholesterol (mg) 0, Sodium (mg) 36
Diabetic Exchanges: *0.5 other carbohydrate, 1 fat*

Chocolate Pecan Mini Cups

These delicate little treats taste like a cross between a pecan pie and a chocolate pie,
combining the best of both worlds. You do need mini muffin pans to make these cups.

MAKES 42 TO 48 MINI CUPS

FILLING:
⅓ cup light brown sugar
1 egg
½ teaspoon vanilla extract
½ cup mini semisweet chocolate chips
½ cup chopped pecans

½ cup (1 stick) margarine, softened
⅓ cup sugar
⅓ cup light brown sugar
1 egg
1 teaspoon vanilla extract
1 cup all-purpose flour
½ teaspoon baking soda

Preheat the oven to 375°F. Coat a miniature muffin pan with nonstick cooking spray.

Prepare the Filling: In a mixing bowl, mix together the brown sugar, egg, and vanilla until thick. Stir in the chocolate chips and pecans, and set aside.

In a mixing bowl, beat together the margarine, sugar, brown sugar, egg, and vanilla. In another bowl, mix together the flour and baking soda, and stir into the margarine mixture just until combined. Put about ½ heaping teaspoon of the mixture in each miniature muffin tin. Bake for 5 to 7 minutes. Spoon some of the Filling over each partially baked cupcake, and continue baking for 8 to 10 minutes until set. Cool in the tins at room temperature, then remove, and serve.

Nutritional Information per Serving (per mini cup)
Calories 66, Protein (g) 1, Carbohydrate (g) 8, Fat (g) 3, Calories from Fat (%) 46, Saturated Fat (g) 1, Dietary Fiber (g) 0, Cholesterol (mg) 9, Sodium (mg) 40
Diabetic Exchanges: *1.5 other carbohydrate, 1.5 fat*

Terrific Tip

WHEN MAKING THESE FABULOUS MINI DESSERTS, EXPERIMENT WITH DIFFERENT MORSELS FROM BUTTERSCOTCH TO WHITE CHOCOLATE. THE NUTS MAY BE OMITTED, OR YOU CAN USE A VARIETY OTHER THAN PECAN.

I took great pride in developing this recipe since Tiramisu is high on my list of favorite desserts.
By using instant espresso powder and reduced-fat cream cheese, you get the indulgence of flavor without the guilt.
Sprinkle with cocoa and chocolate curls before serving. Serve in individual goblets for an amazing display.

MAKES 12 TO 16 SERVINGS

2 egg yolks
6 tablespoons sugar, divided
1 tablespoon plus 1 cup water, divided
2 tablespoons coffee liqueur, divided
2½ teaspoons instant espresso powder, divided
1 (8-ounce) package reduced-fat cream cheese, softened
1 envelope whipped topping mix
½ cup cold skim milk
1 teaspoon vanilla extract
2 (3-ounce) packages lady fingers (24)

In a small pot, mix together the egg yolks, 3 tablespoons of the sugar, 1 tablespoon of the water, 1 tablespoon of the coffee liqueur, and ½ teaspoon of the instant espresso powder. Cook over low heat, whisking constantly, until thickened, about 5 minutes. Remove from the heat, immediately stir in the remaining 1 tablespoon of coffee liqueur, and set aside to cool.

In a microwaveable cup, mix together the remaining 1 cup of water, the remaining 3 tablespoons of sugar, and the remaining 2 teaspoons of espresso powder, and heat in the microwave oven for 30 seconds, or until the sugar is dissolved. Set aside to cool.

In a mixing bowl, beat the cream cheese until creamy. Mix in the cooled, cooked coffee-egg mixture. In another mixing bowl, beat together the whipped topping mix, milk, and vanilla at low speed until blended. Increase the mixer speed to high, and beat until the topping thickens and forms peaks, about 4 minutes. Reserve 1 cup of the whipped topping mixture, and, with a rubber spatula, fold the remaining whipped topping into the coffee-cream cheese mixture.

Split the ladyfingers. In a 9 x 9 x 2-inch dish, place a layer of the ladyfingers across the bottom of the dish. Drizzle with half the espresso mixture, and spread with half the cream cheese mixture. Repeat the layers, beginning with the split ladyfingers and ending with the cream cheese mixture. Spread the reserved 1 cup of the whipped topping mixture in a thin layer on the top. Cover, and refrigerate overnight.

Nutritional Information per Serving
Calories 123, Protein (g) 3, Carbohydrate (g) 14, Fat (g) 5,
Calories from Fat (%) 38, Saturated Fat (g) 3, Dietary Fiber (g) 0,
Cholesterol (mg) 76, Sodium (mg) 84
Diabetic Exchanges: *1 other carbohydrate, 1 fat*

Terrific Tip
TO STORE AN OPEN BOTTLE OF CHAMPAGNE, PUT SOMETHING METAL SUCH AS THE LONG END OF A FORK, KNIFE, OR SPOON INTO THE BOTTLE, AND REFRIGERATE. THIS WILL KEEP THE FIZZ IN THE CHAMPAGNE.

TIRAMISU

Dazzling Toffee Trifle

With convenient ingredients like angel food cake, instant pudding, chocolate, and toffee candy, you don't even have to turn on the oven to put together this dazzling, indulgent sensation.

MAKES 16 SERVINGS

2 (4-serving) packages instant vanilla pudding and pie filling

2½ cups skim milk

1 (16-ounce) store-bought angel food cake, cut into 1½-inch pieces

½ cup almond liqueur

⅓ cup chopped chocolate-covered toffee candy bars

5 tablespoons chocolate syrup, divided

1 (12-ounce) container frozen fat-free whipped topping, thawed

In a mixing bowl, beat or whisk the pudding mix and milk until thick, and set aside. In another bowl, drizzle the cake pieces with the almond liqueur, and let sit for 5 minutes. Add the pudding mixture to the cake pieces, and carefully combine. In a trifle dish or large glass bowl, layer half the cake mixture, top with half the toffee candy, drizzle with 2 tablespoons of the chocolate syrup, and top with half the whipped topping. Repeat the layers with the remaining cake mixture, the remaining toffee candy (reserving 1 tablespoon for topping), 2 tablespoons of the chocolate syrup, and the remaining whipped topping. Sprinkle with the remaining 1 tablespoon of toffee candy, and drizzle with the remaining 1 tablespoon of chocolate syrup.

Nutritional Information per Serving
Calories 224, Protein (g) 3, Carbohydrate (g) 44, Fat (g) 2, Calories from Fat (%) 7, Saturated Fat (g) 1, Dietary Fiber (g) 1, Cholesterol (mg) 3, Sodium (mg) 409
Diabetic Exchanges: *3 other carbohydrate*

Terrific Tip
A TRIFLE BOWL IS A FOOTED GLASS BOWL. IF YOU DON'T HAVE A TRIFLE BOWL, USE A LARGE GLASS BOWL—YOU WANT TO SHOWCASE THE LAYERS TO MAKE A UNIQUE PRESENTATION OF THIS DESSERT.

  ## Banana Cheesecake with Caramel Sauce and Walnuts

Combining America's favorite—cheesecake—with bananas and caramel sauce will put this recipe high on your list. Add ease to your party planning by making this dessert ahead of time. The cheesecake may be prepared up to one day in advance and refrigerated until serving.

MAKES 10 TO 12 SERVINGS

1 cup reduced-fat vanilla wafer crumbs

2 tablespoons margarine, melted

2 (8-ounce) packages reduced-fat cream cheese, softened

1 cup sugar

2 tablespoons cornstarch

2 eggs

1 egg white

1½ cups mashed bananas

1 cup fat-free sour cream

1 tablespoon lemon juice

1 teaspoon vanilla extract

1 teaspoon ground cinnamon

¼ cup coarsely chopped walnuts, toasted (see Terrific Tip, page 22)

2 bananas, sliced

1 (12.25-ounce) jar caramel topping, warmed

Preheat the oven to 350°F. Coat a 9-inch springform pan with nonstick cooking spray. In a small bowl, mix together the vanilla wafer crumbs and margarine, and pat the mixture into the bottom and up the sides of the prepared springform pan.

In another mixing bowl, beat together the cream cheese, sugar, and cornstarch until creamy. Add the eggs and egg white, one at a time, beating after each addition just until blended. Add the mashed bananas, sour cream, lemon juice, vanilla, and cinnamon, mixing until combined. Transfer the filling to the crust-lined springform pan. Bake for 1 hour, or until the center of the cake is just about set. Remove from the oven, and transfer the pan to a wire rack to cool completely at room temperature. Refrigerate until well chilled. To serve, top the cheesecake with the walnuts and sliced bananas, and drizzle with the caramel sauce.

Nutritional Information per Serving
Calories 394, Protein (g) 9, Carbohydrate (g) 60, Fat (g) 13, Calories from Fat (%) 30, Saturated Fat (g) 6, Dietary Fiber (g) 1, Cholesterol (mg) 66, Sodium (mg) 306
Diabetic Exchanges: *1 fruit, 3 other carbohydrate, 2.5 fat*

BLACK RUSSIAN BUNDT CAKE

Black Russian Bundt Cake

Not one person who has tasted this cake failed to "ooh" and "ahh."
It's simple to prepare, with a beautifully rich flavor and a glaze with a kick.

MAKES 16 SERVINGS

1 (18.25-ounce) box yellow cake mix
1 (4-serving) package instant chocolate pudding and pie filling
1 cup nonfat plain yogurt or fat-free sour cream
3/4 cup coffee liqueur, divided
2/3 cup skim milk
1/4 cup canola oil
1/4 cup vodka
1 egg
3 egg whites
1/2 cup confectioners' sugar

Preheat the oven to 350°F. Coat a 10-inch Bundt pan with nonstick cooking spray.

In a mixing bowl, combine the cake mix, pudding mix, yogurt, 1/4 cup of the coffee liqueur, milk, oil, vodka, egg, and egg whites, blending until mixed. Pour into the prepared Bundt pan, and bake for 40 to 50 minutes, or until an inserted toothpick comes out clean.

Meanwhile, prepare the glaze. In a small bowl, mix together the confectioners' sugar and the remaining 1/2 cup of coffee liqueur, and set aside.

Cool the cake in the pan on a wire rack for 10 minutes before inverting onto a serving plate. Prick holes with a toothpick all over the top of the cake, and spoon the glaze over the top. Cool at room temperature before serving, if you can wait that long!

Nutritional Information per Serving
Calories 273, Protein (g) 4, Carbohydrate (g) 43, Fat (g) 7, Calories from Fat (%) 22, Saturated Fat (g) 1, Dietary Fiber (g) 0, Cholesterol (mg) 14, Sodium (mg) 338
Diabetic Exchanges: *3 other carbohydrate, 1.5 fat*

Terrific Tip

USE A DECORATIVE BUNDT PAN, SUCH AS ONE SHAPED AS A ROSE, FOR A PICTURE PERFECT BUNDT CAKE. GARNISHES CAN CONSIST OF WHATEVER YOU HAVE IN YOUR KITCHEN. I, FOR EXAMPLE, WENT INTO MY BACKYARD AND PICKED KUMQUATS TO LAY AROUND THE BASE OF THE CAKE.

Terrific Tip
PULL THAT DEVILED EGG DISH OUT OF THE CLOSET
AND FILL EACH SECTION WITH DIFFERENT COFFEE
CONDIMENTS: WHITE CHOCOLATE CHIPS, BROWN
SUGAR, CANDIED ORANGE SLICES, CHOCOLATE
CHIPS, CINNAMON STICKS, AND COLORED SUGAR.
FILL THE CENTER SECTION WITH WHIPPED TOPPING.

Berry Trifle

With layers of cake, custard, and berries, enhanced with a hint of orange and combined in a magnificent presentation, this trifle is a winner! I am partial to homemade custard, but instant vanilla pudding may be substituted for a speedy version. Make ahead, and refrigerate until serving.

MAKES 16 SERVINGS

1/2 cup sugar

1/3 cup cornstarch

3 cups skim milk

2 egg yolks, slightly beaten

1 teaspoon vanilla extract

1 (10 3/4-ounce) frozen,
   reduced-fat pound cake, thawed

1/4 cup seedless raspberry jam

1/3 cup orange liqueur or orange juice

2 pints raspberries, sliced strawberries,
   or blueberries, divided

1 (8-ounce) container frozen fat-free
   whipped topping, thawed

2 tablespoons sliced almonds, toasted
   (see Terrific Tip, page 22)

In a medium saucepan, stir together the sugar and cornstarch. Gradually add the milk, stirring until smooth. Stir in the beaten egg yolks. Cook over medium heat, stirring constantly, until the mixture comes to a boil. Reduce the heat, boil gently for 2 minutes, and remove from the heat. Transfer to a bowl, stir in the vanilla, and refrigerate until chilled.

Cut the pound cake into 1-inch slices. Arrange half of the slices on bottom of a trifle bowl or a deep glass bowl. Spread the raspberry jam over the slices, and drizzle with the orange liqueur. Layer with half the berries, half the chilled custard, and half the whipped topping. Repeat the layers with the remaining ingredients, beginning with the pound cake and ending with the whipped topping. Top with the toasted almonds.

Nutritional Information per Serving
Calories 181, Protein (g) 3, Carbohydrate (g) 36, Fat (g) 2, Calories from Fat (%) 8, Saturated Fat (g) 0, Dietary Fiber (g) 2, Cholesterol (mg) 27, Sodium (mg) 98
Diabetic Exchanges: *0.5 fruit, 2 other carbohydrate, 0.5 fat*

ALMOND CHOCOLATE SANDIES, CHOCOLATE PECAN MINI CUPS and CHOCOLATE COVERED STRAWBERRIES

Holiday Dinner

Even though most of us plan official holiday dinners only about twice a year, there is more preparation and enthusiasm associated with this type of meal than with any other. With an emphasis on tradition, key ingredients appear on most holiday tables, and I have updated these classics. There's no turkey dish on this menu, simply because I find that in every family, there's always someone who has his or her own special, secret turkey recipe. I prefer to devote my time to preparing sensational sides that often steal the show. The Sweet Potato, Pecan, and Cranberry Surprise and the Stuffed Acorn Squash are both instantly appealing and savory recipes. And there's always room for dessert! Pecan pie, gingerbread, and Yule log are popular holiday indulgences. I admit I overeat every holiday, but with this selection of Trim & Terrific™ recipes, the only plump thing at your home will be the turkey.

MENU SELECTIONS

EXCITING EXTRAS

▶ Dress up your holiday table with a vase of red roses, accented with a few white lilies or lighter colored roses.

▶ Use creative, holiday-themed serving plate holders.

▶ Set the table with your finest tablecloth, dishes, silver, and linen napkins. What better time than during the holidays to make your very best presentation?

▶ Different sized candles can add visual interest to your holiday setting.

▶ Use fanned strawberry slices as extra garnish on desserts.

▶ When cranberries are in season, fill a vase with berries for a decorative touch.

Short Cuts

- Order a cooked turkey, and garnish it at home with fresh parsley and crab apples to give it a personal touch, or order a honey-baked ham.
- Create a lovely, easy centerpiece by filling a glass bowl with pomegranates.
- To save time during the very busy holiday season, prepare some recipes ahead of time and store them in the freezer.
- Order festive holiday cookies or pies from your favorite bakery.
- For extra-quick clean up, purchase holiday-themed paper goods to use when serving dessert.

STUFFED ACORN SQUASH

ASPARAGUS PROCIUTTO BUNDLES

Sweet Potato, Pecan, and Cranberry Surprise

When you use a food processor to slice the potatoes, this is one of the simplest and most impressive recipes you can serve.
I promise a picture-perfect presentation every time as the foil keeps the potatoes from sticking and dish inverts with ease.

MAKES 8 SERVINGS

2/3 cup dried cranberries
1/3 cup chopped pecans
1/3 cup light brown sugar
3 tablespoons margarine, melted
1 teaspoon ground cinnamon
1/2 teaspoon ground nutmeg
2 pounds sweet potatoes (yams)

Preheat the oven to 400°F. Line a 9-inch round cake pan with aluminum foil, and coat with nonstick cooking spray.

In a small bowl, mix together the cranberries, pecans, brown sugar, melted margarine, cinnamon, and nutmeg, and set aside. Peel the sweet potatoes, and slice very thin (preferably with a food processor and the slicing attachment). Spoon one-third of the cranberry mixture on the bottom of the prepared cake pan. Arrange one-third of the potato slices in concentric circles, overlapping in the bottom of the pan. Spread another one-third of the cranberry mixture over the potatoes. Top with another one-third of the potato slices, arranged in concentric circles. Top with the remaining one-third of the cranberry mixture, and repeat arranging the potato slices on top.

Coat a sheet of aluminum foil with nonstick cooking spray, and tightly place it over the potatoes. Bake for 45 minutes, remove the foil, and continue baking for another 20 minutes, or until brown and crisp on top and the potatoes are tender. Place a serving plate or cake plate on top of the cake pan, and invert immediately. Remove the foil from top, and serve.

Nutritional Information per Serving
Calories 252, Protein (g) 2, Carbohydrate (g) 46, Fat (g) 8, Calories from Fat (%) 27,
Saturated Fat (g) 1, Dietary Fiber (g) 5, Cholesterol (mg) 0, Sodium (mg) 93
Diabetic Exchanges: *2 starch, 0.5 fruit, 0.5 other carbohydrate, 1 fat*

Stuffed Acorn Squash

If you have never experienced acorn squash, don't pass on this recipe—it's outstanding. This fabulous dish requires some time to make, so prepare it the day before and refrigerate. Before serving, bake it in the oven at 350°F until heated through.

MAKES 6 SERVINGS

1 (6-ounce) package long grain
  and wild rice mix
3 (10- to 12-ounce) acorn squashes,
  cut into halves and seeded
2 tablespoons margarine
1 cup chopped onion
2 tablespoons lemon juice
2 teaspoons dried sage leaves
1/2 cup dried cranberries
1/4 cup chopped walnuts, toasted
  (see Terrific Tip, page 22)
2 tablespoons light brown sugar
Salt and pepper, to taste

Preheat the oven to 375°F. Coat a baking sheet with nonstick cooking spray. Prepare the rice according to the package directions, and set aside.

Arrange the squash halves cut-side down on the prepared baking sheet. Bake for 40 minutes, or until tender. Reduce the oven temperature to 350°F. Scoop out the squash pulp, carefully leaving a 1/4-inch shell. Place the pulp in a small bowl.

In a skillet, heat the margarine over medium heat. Add the onion, and cook, stirring, until tender, 3 to 5 minutes. Stir in the cooked rice, squash pulp, lemon juice, and sage, mixing well and breaking up the squash pulp into smaller pieces. Stir in the cranberries, walnuts, and brown sugar. Divide the stuffing to fill the acorn squash shells. Place the shells on the baking sheet. (You may have to trim a bit off the bottom of some of the shells to help them stand upright.) Bake for 15 minutes, or until heated through. Season with salt and pepper.

Nutritional Information per Serving
Calories 271, Protein (g) 5, Carbohydrate (g) 49, Fat (g) 8, Calories from Fat (%) 24,
Saturated Fat (g) 1, Dietary Fiber (g) 4, Cholesterol (mg) 0, Sodium (mg) 471
Diabetic Exchanges: *2.5 starch, 0.5 fruit, 1 fat*

Asparagus Prosciutto Bundles

This elegant, simple side can be made ahead of time, covered with plastic wrap, and refrigerated until ready to bake.
The unique and distinct flavors of goat cheese, prosciutto, and asparagus merge together for a lively taste.
These bundles also make a delicious, easy-to-eat option for a cocktail buffet.

MAKES 10 TO 12 BUNDLES

1 pound thin asparagus spears, trimmed
3 ounces prosciutto ham slices
2 1/2 ounces herb and garlic goat cheese

Preheat the oven to 400°F.

Cook the asparagus in a large pot of boiling water or in a microwave oven until crisp tender, about 5 minutes. Transfer the asparagus to a bowl of ice water, and pat dry. Divide the prosciutto slices, and spread each slice with about 1/2 teaspoon of the cheese. Place a few asparagus in each slice of prosciutto, and wrap tightly around the spears. Transfer to a baking sheet, and bake until heated through, about 5 minutes. Transfer to a serving dish, and serve warm or at room temperature.

Nutritional Information per Serving (per bundle)
Calories 38, Protein (g) 3, Carbohydrate (g) 2, Fat (g) 2, Calories from Fat (%) 47,
Saturated Fat (g) 1, Dietary Fiber (g) 1, Cholesterol (mg) 9, Sodium (mg) 148
Diabetic Exchanges: *1 vegetable, 0.5 fat*

Peas and Mushrooms

I always like to include peas as a colorful and nutritious holiday side dish.

MAKES 4 TO 6 SERVINGS

1 (16-ounce) package frozen peas
1 tablespoon margarine
1/4 cup chopped onion
1 cup sliced fresh portabella or plain
  mushrooms
Salt and pepper, to taste

Cook the peas according to package directions, drain, and set aside. In a small skillet, melt the margarine over medium heat. Add the onion and mushrooms, and cook, stirring, until tender, about 5 minutes. Combine the onion and mushrooms with the peas, season with salt and pepper, and serve.

Nutritional Information per Serving
Calories 81, Protein (g) 4, Carbohydrate (g) 11, Fat (g) 2, Calories from Fat (%) 24, Saturated Fat (g) 0, Dietary Fiber (g) 4, Cholesterol (mg) 0, Sodium (mg) 107
Diabetic Exchanges: *1 starch*

Wild Rice Fruit Pilaf

Wild and brown rice give this rich pilaf a nutritional boost, the dried fruit adds a touch of sweetness, and the walnuts give it a toasty crunch. When you are running out of oven space, select this tasty side dish since it's prepared on the stovetop.

MAKES 10 TO 12 SERVINGS

1 tablespoon margarine
1/2 cup chopped onion
6 cups canned beef broth
1 1/4 cups wild rice
1 1/4 cups brown rice
1 cup dried cranberries, cherries,
  or a mixture
1/4 cup sherry
1 cup sliced green onions (scallions)
1/2 cup chopped fresh parsley
1/3 cup walnut halves, toasted
  (see Terrific Tip, page 22)
1 teaspoon dried thyme leaves
Salt and pepper, to taste

In a large pot over medium heat, melt the margarine. Add the onion, and cook, stirring, until tender, 3 to 5 minutes. Add the beef broth, wild rice, and brown rice, and bring to a boil. Reduce the heat, cover, and simmer until the rice is tender, 45 to 60 minutes.

Meanwhile, in a small bowl, add the dried fruit and sherry, let sit for 10 minutes, and drain the fruit (see Terrific Tip). When the rice is done, stir in the reserved fruit, green onions, parsley, walnuts, thyme, salt, and pepper.

Nutritional Information per Serving
Calories 204, Protein (g) 7, Carbohydrate (g) 37, Fat (g) 4, Calories from Fat (%) 16, Saturated Fat (g) 0, Dietary Fiber (g) 3, Cholesterol (mg) 0, Sodium (mg) 517
Diabetic Exchanges: *2 starch, 0.5 fruit, 0.5 fat*

Terrific Tip
IF YOU LIKE THE TASTE OF SHERRY, THERE IS NO NEED TO DRAIN THE DRIED FRUIT AFTER SOAKING—YOU CAN ADD THE SHERRY TO THE COOKED RICE ALONG WITH THE FRUIT.

STUFFED
ACORN SQUASH

Cornbread Dressing

Every holiday table should include cornbread dressing, in my opinion, and this recipe has proven to be my guests' absolute favorite. It all begins with just a pan of cornbread, but you can dress up this basic recipe by adding other ingredients from cooked wild rice to cooked sausage or chopped apples before baking it in the oven. When making this dish ahead of time, refrigerate until needed, and then allow it to warm to room temperature before baking.

MAKES 8 TO 10 SERVINGS

2 (8½-ounce) boxes corn muffin mix
4 eggs, divided
⅔ cup skim milk
8 slices white bread, toasted and
  crusts removed
1 cup chopped onion
1 cup chopped celery
2 egg whites, slightly beaten
2 cups canned chicken broth
1 teaspoon poultry seasoning
Pinch sugar
Salt and pepper, to taste
1 bunch green onions (scallions), sliced

Preheat the oven to 350°F. Coat a 13 x 9 x 2-inch baking pan with nonstick cooking spray. Coat a 2-quart baking dish with nonstick cooking spray.

Prepare the corn muffin mix with 2 of the eggs and the milk, and bake in the prepared 13 x 9 x 2-inch pan according to the package directions. When cooled, crumble the cornbread, and set aside. Crumble the white bread, and set aside.

Coat a small skillet with nonstick cooking spray, and set over medium heat. Add the onion and celery, and cook, stirring, until tender, 5 to 7 minutes. In a large bowl, combine the crumbled corn bread and white bread, sautéed vegetables, the remaining 2 slightly beaten eggs, the egg whites, chicken broth, poultry seasoning, sugar, salt, and pepper, mixing well. Transfer to the prepared 2-quart baking dish. Sprinkle the green onions on top. Bake for 45 minutes, or until heated through.

Nutritional Information per Serving
Calories 309, Protein (g) 10, Carbohydrate (g) 47, Fat (g) 9, Calories from Fat (%) 26, Saturated Fat (g) 2, Dietary Fiber (g) 4, Cholesterol (mg) 86, Sodium (mg) 790
Diabetic Exchanges: *3 starch, 1 fat*

GLAZED HAM WITH PECAN CRUST

Glazed Ham with Pecan Crust

There's no need to buy a honey-baked ham at the store! This stunning ham has incredible flavor, yet it's so simple to prepare. The leftovers make the best sandwiches.

MAKES 20 TO 25 SERVINGS

1 (10-pound) fully cooked, bone-in ham
2 cups apple cider
1½ cups finely chopped pecans
1 cup light brown sugar
1 tablespoon Dijon mustard

Terrific Tip
GARNISH THE HAM WITH CRAB APPLES OR POMEGRANATES WHILE THEY ARE IN SEASON.

Preheat the oven to 325°F.

Insert a meat thermometer into the center of the ham without touching the bone. Place the ham in a baking dish, and pour the cider over. Roast in the oven, basting with cider every 30 minutes, for a total cooking time of 12 to 15 minutes per pound, or until the thermometer registers 140°F.

Meanwhile, in a bowl, combine the pecans, brown sugar, and mustard. Remove the ham from the oven about 40 minutes before it's done cooking, and firmly pat the sugar-pecan mixture all over the ham. Return to the oven, and continue roasting until the crust is brown and the ham is done. Slice the ham, and serve with sauce—some of the topping falls into the cider in the pan, making a sauce that is the perfect accompaniment to the ham.

Nutritional Information per Serving
Calories 306, Protein (g) 35, Carbohydrate (g) 12, Fat (g) 13, Calories from Fat (%) 38, Saturated Fat (g) 3, Dietary Fiber (g) 1, Cholesterol (mg) 75, Sodium (mg) 1824
Diabetic Exchanges: *5 lean meat, 1 other carbohydrate*

Pecan Pie with Honey Crunch Topping

For the most incredible pecan pie ever, splurge with the Honey Crunch Topping.
For a chocolate variation, add ½ to 1 cup semisweet chocolate chips to the pie filling before baking.

MAKES 8 TO 10 SERVINGS

3 eggs
½ cup light brown sugar
¼ cup sugar
1 cup light corn syrup
2 tablespoons margarine, melted
1 tablespoon vanilla extract
1 cup chopped pecans
1 (9-inch) unbaked pie shell
Honey Crunch Topping
  (recipe follows, optional)

Preheat the oven to 350°F.

In a mixing bowl, beat together the eggs, brown sugar, and sugar until creamy. Add the corn syrup, margarine, and vanilla, mixing well. Stir in the pecans. Pour into the pie shell, and bake for 40 to 50 minutes, or until the pie is set.

Nutritional Information per Serving (without Honey Crunch Topping)
Calories 346, Protein (g) 4, Carbohydrate (g) 50, Fat (g) 16, Calories from Fat (%) 40,
Saturated Fat (g) 3, Dietary Fiber (g) 1, Cholesterol (mg) 66, Sodium (mg) 38
Diabetic Exchanges: *3.5 other carbohydrate, 3 fat*

Honey Crunch Topping

Indulge by adding this fabulous topping to your Pecan Pie, and you'll earn bragging rights for years to come.
It is never too late to include this incredible topping, as it is added in the last five minutes of baking.

MAKES TOPPING FOR 1 (9-INCH) PIE, 8 TO 10 SERVINGS

⅓ cup light brown sugar
3 tablespoons margarine
3 tablespoons honey
1½ cups pecan halves

In a medium saucepan, combine the brown sugar, margarine, and honey. Cook over low heat, stirring constantly, until the sugar dissolves. Add the pecans, and stir until well coated. During last 5 minutes of baking the Pecan Pie, remove the pie from the oven, and spread the crunch topping evenly over the top. Turn on the broiler, return the pie to the oven, and broil until the topping is bubbly and golden brown, watching carefully.

Nutritional Information per Serving
Calories 189, Protein (g) 2, Carbohydrate (g) 15, Fat (g) 15, Calories from Fat (%) 68,
Saturated Fat (g) 2, Dietary Fiber (g) 2, Cholesterol (mg) 0, Sodium (mg) 43
Diabetic Exchanges: *1 other carbohydrate, 3 fat*

CRANBERRY CAKE WITH VANILLA SAUCE

Cranberry Cake with Vanilla Sauce

This recipe takes full advantage of cranberry season. I usually cut the cake into squares and drizzle it with the Vanilla Sauce.

MAKES 30 TO 35 SQUARES

4 tablespoons margarine, melted
3/4 cup sugar
3/4 cup light brown sugar
2 cups all-purpose flour
1 1/2 teaspoons baking soda
1 (12-ounce) can fat-free evaporated milk
2 cups chopped fresh cranberries,
   or 1 1/2 cups dried cranberries
1/2 cup chopped walnuts (optional)
Vanilla Sauce (recipe follows)

VANILLA SAUCE:
1/3 cup sugar
1/3 cup fat-free evaporated milk
3 tablespoons margarine
1 teaspoon vanilla extract

Preheat the oven to 350°F. Coat a 13 x 9 x 2-inch baking pan with nonstick cooking spray.

In a large mixing bowl, beat the margarine, sugar, and brown sugar. In another bowl, mix together the flour and baking soda. Gradually add the flour mixture to the margarine mixture alternately with the milk, mixing thoroughly after each addition. Fold in the cranberries and walnuts, if desired. Pour the batter into the prepared baking pan. Bake for 20 to 25 minutes, or just until the top springs back when touched. Cut into squares, and serve warm with the Vanilla Sauce.

Vanilla Sauce: In a small saucepan, combine the sugar, evaporated milk, and margarine, and bring to a boil. Boil for 4 to 5 minutes, or until slightly thickened. Remove from the heat, and mix in the vanilla. Serve warm over the Cranberry Cake.

Nutritional Information per Serving
Calories 114, Protein (g) 2, Carbohydrate (g) 21, Fat (g) 2,
Calories from Fat (%) 19, Saturated Fat (g) 0,
Dietary Fiber (g) 1, Cholesterol (mg) 1, Sodium (mg) 97
Diabetic Exchanges: *1 other carbohydrate, 0.5 fat*

Terrific Tip
WHEN CRANBERRIES ARE IN SEASON, BUY EXTRA AND FREEZE FOR UP TO ONE YEAR TO ENJOY FRESH CRANBERRIES ALL YEAR LONG.

Chocolate Yule Log with Coconut Cream Filling

If you like the taste of Mounds candy bars, this classic holiday recipe has your name on it! Don't let the various steps of this recipe fool you into thinking it's complicated. It's really quite simple to make the cake roll ahead of time, then later add the filling and icing for a very impressive dessert. I occasionally toss some pecans (one of my favorites) into the filling.

MAKES 16 TO 20 SERVINGS

1 egg
6 tablespoons water, divided
1 cup sugar
1 teaspoon vanilla extract
3/4 cup all-purpose flour
1/4 cup cocoa
1 teaspoon baking powder
3 egg whites
2 tablespoons confectioners' sugar
Coconut Cream Filling (recipe follows)
Chocolate Frosting (recipe follows)
Fresh mint sprigs and cranberries,
   for garnish

COCONUT CREAM FILLING:

1/3 cup sugar
3 tablespoons cornstarch
1 1/2 cups skim milk
1 egg yolk
1/2 cup flaked coconut
1 ounce reduced-fat cream cheese
1 teaspoon vanilla extract
1 teaspoon coconut extract

CHOCOLATE FROSTING:

1 (16-ounce) box confectioners' sugar
1/3 cup cocoa
3 tablespoons margarine, softened
1 to 2 tablespoons skim milk

Preheat the oven to 375°F. Coat a 15 x 10 x 1-inch jelly-roll pan with nonstick cooking spray. Line the pan with wax paper, and coat the wax paper with nonstick cooking spray.

In a mixing bowl, beat the egg with 2 tablespoons of the water until thick and pale colored, for about 2 minutes. Gradually add the sugar, vanilla, and remaining 4 tablespoons of water, beating well. In another mixing bowl, mix together the flour, cocoa, and baking powder, and add to the egg mixture, stirring until blended. In another mixing bowl, beat the egg whites until stiff peaks form (see Terrific Tip, page 76). With a rubber spatula, gradually fold the egg whites into the chocolate mixture.

Spread the batter evenly in the prepared pan. Bake for 12 to 15 minutes, or until the cake springs back when touched lightly in the center. Immediately loosen the cake from the sides of the pan, and invert onto a towel dusted with the confectioners' sugar. Peel off the wax paper. Starting at the short end of the cake, roll up the towel and cake together. Set aside to cool completely at room temperature.

Carefully unroll the cake, and remove the towel. Spread the Coconut Cream Filling over the cake and roll up jelly-roll fashion. Place the cake on a serving platter, seam side down, cover with plastic wrap to hold in place, and chill in the refrigerator for 1 hour. Frost both ends and the log with the Chocolate Frosting. Use a fork to lightly mark the log to look like a tree. Garnish with fresh mint sprigs and cranberries for holiday flair.

Coconut Cream Filling: In a medium pot, combine the sugar and cornstarch. Stir in the milk and egg yolk. Set over medium heat, and cook, stirring constantly, until thickened and bubbly, about 5 minutes. Remove from the heat, and stir in the coconut, cream cheese, vanilla, and coconut extract. Cool completely in the refrigerator before using.

Chocolate Frosting: In a mixing bowl, mix together the confectioners' sugar, cocoa, and margarine. Gradually stir in enough milk to form a spreadable consistency. Use the frosting right away.

Nutritional Information per Serving
Calories 226, Protein (g) 3, Carbohydrate (g) 46, Fat (g) 4, Calories from Fat (%) 15, Saturated Fat (g) 2, Dietary Fiber (g) 1, Cholesterol (mg) 23, Sodium (mg) 81
Diabetic Exchanges: *3 other carbohydrate, 1 fat*

Terrific Tip
USE FESTIVE BERRY NAPKIN RING HOLDERS
TO HOLD VOTIVE CANDLES.

Gingerbread Squares

My sister Ilene insists that I include a gingerbread recipe on my menu, for the holidays aren't complete without the traditional flavor of ginger and cinnamon. These fabulous, moist squares will quickly disappear as your guests savor their spicy goodness.

MAKES 25 SQUARES

1¼ cups all-purpose flour
1 teaspoon ground ginger
1 teaspoon ground cinnamon
½ teaspoon baking soda
½ cup molasses
½ cup sugar
½ cup (1 stick) margarine, melted
½ cup buttermilk
1 egg
1 tablespoon confectioners' sugar

Preheat the oven to 350°F. Coat a 9 x 9 x 2-inch baking pan with nonstick cooking spray.

In a small bowl, mix together the flour, ginger, cinnamon, and baking soda, and set aside. In another bowl, combine the molasses, sugar, melted margarine, buttermilk, and egg, and whisk to blend. Stir in the flour mixture. Transfer the batter to the prepared baking pan, and bake for 20 to 25 minutes, or until an inserted toothpick comes out clean. Sprinkle with the confectioners' sugar. Cut into squares, and serve warm or at room temperature.

Nutritional Information per Serving (per square)
Calories 95, Protein (g) 1, Carbohydrate (g) 14, Fat (g) 4, Calories from Fat (%) 37, Saturated Fat (g) 1, Dietary Fiber (g) 0, Cholesterol (mg) 9, Sodium (mg) 78
Diabetic Exchanges: *1 other carbohydrate, 1 fat*

Souper Bowl Party

You may associate the celebrations and crowds of January with New Year's Eve, but my mind is already on Super Bowl Sunday. The Super Bowl game is one of the most anticipated and widely viewed sporting events of the year. People bet on everything from who wins the coin toss to who ultimately wins the game, but the only sure bet is that everyone loves a good Super Bowl party. I like to call my football fiesta a "Souper Bowl" party, because, during the cold month of January, a soup buffet is the perfect way to feed an energetic crowd. Prepare a pot of hearty soup like Beef and Barley French Onion or give your guests a choice of two varieties. Serve soups simmering on the stove, or use crockpots to maintain the ideal temperature. Since some people don't want to miss the commercials and others insist on seeing every second of the game, have mugs by the soup so guests can eat at their leisure. I always have a few appetizers and simple desserts scattered around so that I don't lose my place on the sofa by spending too much time in the kitchen!

MENU SELECTIONS

EXCITING EXTRAS

▶ Serve soup in tureens.
▶ Accessorize and decorate with team theme and colors.
▶ Pick up a bunch of flowers, and arrange simply in a vase to create a fun, casual decoration.

97

Short Cuts

▷ Prepare the soups ahead of time, and freeze until the big day.

▷ Serve the soups directly from pots on the stovetop.

▷ Pick up assorted cheeses, and decorate with grapes and other fruits for easy and nutritious appetizers.

▷ Purchase a hearty salad from your local supermarket, and serve with your favorite bottled dressing and bread.

▷ Make a quick trip to the bakery to buy assorted cookies.

Stromboli

This easily-prepared, baked sandwich is the perfect quick bite and a guaranteed hit. I use frozen bread dough so there's no time-consuming yeast involved. Toss in olives, jalapeño peppers, or any other seasonings to create your personal variation. People of all ages love these strombolis, and the kids grab them right out of the oven even faster than the adults. This recipe works great as an appetizer, or served with soup.

MAKES 12 SLICES

1 (16-ounce) frozen bread dough, thawed
4 ounces thinly sliced ham
1/2 teaspoon dried basil leaves, divided
1/2 teaspoon dried oregano leaves, divided
3 ounces sliced provolone cheese
1 cup shredded part-skim mozzarella cheese

Preheat the oven to 375°F. Coat a baking sheet with nonstick cooking spray.

Pat the bread dough into an approximately 10 x 15-inch rectangle on the prepared baking sheet. Arrange the ham slices lengthwise down the center. Sprinkle with ¼ teaspoon of the basil and ¼ teaspoon of the oregano. Arrange the provolone slices over the seasonings, sprinkle with the mozzarella and the remaining basil and oregano. Bring the long edges of the rectangle to the center and press the edges to seal. Seal the ends. Invert so that the seam side is down on the baking sheet. Bake for 20 to 22 minutes, or until light brown.

Nutritional Information per Serving (per slice)
Calories 166, Protein (g) 10, Carbohydrate (g) 20, Fat (g) 6, Calories from Fat (%) 30, Saturated Fat (g) 2, Dietary Fiber (g) 1, Cholesterol (mg) 15, Sodium (mg) 452
Diabetic Exchanges: *1 medium-fat meat, 1.5 starch*

Nachos with a Flair

Nachos have withstood the test of time and are still a favorite recipe to serve during the Super Bowl and beyond. Great flavors merge together to give this winner new spunk. Serve with a dollop of fat-free sour cream, if desired.

MAKES 8 TO 12 SERVINGS

3/4 cup red spaghetti sauce
3 tablespoons hoisin sauce
2 to 3 tablespoons Asian chili sauce
1 teaspoon minced garlic
1 (8-ounce) bag baked tortilla chips
1 cup shredded reduced-fat sharp
  Cheddar cheese
1 cup shredded reduced-fat Monterey
  Jack cheese

Preheat the oven to 500°F.

In a small bowl, mix together the spaghetti sauce, hoisin sauce, Asian chili sauce to taste (depending on how hot you like it), and garlic. On a baking sheet, spread the tortilla chips. Sprinkle with all of the Cheddar cheese, top evenly with the sauce, and then sprinkle with the Monterey Jack cheese. Bake for 3 to 5 minutes, or until the cheese melts. Watch closely.

Nutritional Information per Serving
Calories 138, Protein (g) 7, Carbohydrate (g) 19, Fat (g) 4, Calories from Fat (%) 26, Saturated Fat (g) 2, Dietary Fiber (g) 2, Cholesterol (mg) 10, Sodium (mg) 322
Diabetic Exchanges: *1 lean meat, 1.5 starch*

Halibut Pâté

This light, mild dip emerges from a flavorful combination of halibut, dill, and a dash of hot sauce. Serve with crackers or crostini.

MAKES ABOUT 16 (2-TABLESPOON) SERVINGS

1/2 cup water
1/2 cup white wine
1/4 cup grated carrot
2 1/2 teaspoons minced onion, divided
12 ounces halibut filet
1 (8-ounce) package reduced-fat cream
  cheese, softened
2 tablespoons lemon juice
1 teaspoon Worcestershire sauce
1/2 teaspoon salt
1/4 teaspoon minced garlic
1/4 teaspoon dried dill weed leaves
Hot pepper sauce, to taste
Fresh parsley and lemon wedges, for garnish

In a pan, combine the water, wine, carrot, and 1 teaspoon of the minced onion, add the halibut, bring to a simmer, and poach until the fish is done and flaky, 15 to 20 minutes. Remove the fish from the pan, and cool. When cool, flake the halibut, and set aside.

In a food processor or mixer, combine the cream cheese, lemon juice, Worcestershire sauce, salt, garlic, dill weed, hot pepper sauce, and remaining 1 1/2 teaspoons of minced onion, mixing until smooth. Fold in the halibut. Refrigerate for 3 or 4 hours, or overnight before serving. Serve with fresh parsley and lemon wedges.

Nutritional Information per Serving
Calories 60, Protein (g) 6, Carbohydrate (g) 1, Fat (g) 4, Calories from Fat (%) 55, Saturated Fat (g) 2, Dietary Fiber (g) 0, Cholesterol (mg) 17, Sodium (mg) 148
Diabetic Exchanges: *1 medium-fat meat*

> **Terrific Tip**
> POACH IS A TERM FOR COOKING FOOD (SUCH AS FISH) BY SUBMERGING IT IN VERY GENTLY BOILING LIQUID.

Walnut and Spinach Cheese Bread

There's no need to grab for the butter because a slice of this bread, warm from the oven, simply melts in your mouth.
The wonderful blend of walnuts, spinach, and cheese make it hard to resist. This bread is the perfect match to a cup of hot soup.

MAKES 16 SERVINGS

2½ cups all-purpose flour
2 tablespoons sugar
2 teaspoons baking powder
½ teaspoon baking soda
½ teaspoon ground dry mustard
Dash cayenne
¼ cup canola oil
1 cup shredded reduced-fat sharp
  Cheddar cheese
1 cup buttermilk
1 egg, slightly beaten
1 cup fresh baby spinach
⅔ cup chopped walnuts

Preheat the oven to 350°F. Coat a 9 x 5 x 3-inch loaf pan with nonstick cooking spray.

In a bowl, mix together the flour, sugar, baking powder, baking soda, dry mustard, and cayenne. Add the oil, and work together with a pastry blender or fingertips. Stir in the cheese. In a small bowl, blend together the buttermilk and egg, and stir into the flour mixture just until moistened. Mix in the spinach and walnuts. Transfer to the prepared loaf pan. Bake for 40 minutes, or until the top is lightly browned. Serve warm or at room temperature.

Nutritional Information per Serving
Calories 173, Protein (g) 6, Carbohydrate (g) 18, Fat (g) 9, Calories from Fat (%) 45,
Saturated Fat (g) 2, Dietary Fiber (g) 1, Cholesterol (mg) 18, Sodium (mg) 167
Diabetic Exchanges: *1 starch, 2 fat*

Beef and Barley French Onion Soup

This is a hearty, full-flavored soup with meat, mushrooms, and a rich beef broth that is stress-free to prepare.
If preferred, you don't even have to top it with the French bread and cheese—the soup is fabulous either way.

MAKES 8 TO 10 SERVINGS

2 onions, halved and thinly sliced
  (about 4 cups)
2 pounds boneless sirloin steak,
  trimmed of fat and cut into chunks
½ pound sliced fresh mushrooms
¼ pound fresh shiitake mushrooms,
  stems removed
1 teaspoon minced garlic
1 teaspoon light brown sugar
4 cups canned beef broth
2 (10½-ounce) cans beef consommé
2 cups water
¾ cup pearl barley
3 tablespoons reduced-sodium soy sauce
¼ cup dry sherry, optional
10 thinly sliced pieces French bread, toasted
1½ cups shredded reduced-fat Swiss
  cheese (or use slices)

Coat a large pot with nonstick cooking spray, and set over medium-high heat. Add the onions, and cook, stirring occasionally, until lightly browned, about 15 minutes. Add the meat, fresh mushrooms, shiitake mushrooms, garlic, and brown sugar, and cook, stirring, until the mushrooms are tender and the meat is browned, 10 to 12 minutes. Add the beef broth, consommé, water, and barley. Bring to a boil, lower the heat, cover, and simmer until the barley and meat are tender, 50 minutes to 1 hour. Add the soy sauce and sherry, and cook for 5 more minutes. To serve, ladle the hot soup into a mug or cup, top with a slice of French bread and some cheese.

Nutritional Information per Serving
Calories 353, Protein (g) 34, Carbohydrate (g) 34, Fat (g) 8,
Calories from Fat (%) 21, Saturated Fat (g) 4, Dietary Fiber (g) 4,
Cholesterol (mg) 64, Sodium (mg) 1182
Diabetic Exchanges: *3.5 lean meat, 2 starch, 1 vegetable*

Terrific Tip
SHIITAKE MUSHROOMS HAVE A DISTINCTIVE, SMOKY FLAVOR. THE TOUGH STEM MUST BE REMOVED BEFORE USING. THEY ARE ALSO AVAILABLE DRIED IN ASIAN MARKETS. IF DESIRED, YOU CAN OMIT THEM FROM THIS RECIPE, AND INCREASE THE QUANTITY OF FRESH PLAIN MUSHROOMS TO ¾ CUP—I INCLUDE THE SHIITAKES BECAUSE THEY ADD TEXTURE AND FLAVOR TO THE SOUP.

Potato Soup

Here's a smooth and creamy comfort food that pleases everyone. Have ready small bowls of reduced-fat cheeses, green onions, and nonfat sour cream so each guest can dress up their own bowl. This soup is simple, but it always gets tons of compliments.

MAKES 8 (1-CUP) SERVINGS

6 baking potatoes, peeled and
  cubed (6 cups)
1/2 cup sliced carrots
5 to 6 cups fat-free chicken broth or
  vegetable broth, divided
1 tablespoon margarine
1 cup finely chopped onion
1 1/2 cups skim milk
Dash hot pepper sauce
Salt and pepper, to taste
Chopped green onions (scallions)

In a large pot, boil the potatoes and carrots in 4 cups of the broth, covered, until the potatoes are tender, about 20 minutes. Meanwhile, add the margarine to a small skillet over medium heat. Add the onion, and cook, stirring, until tender, 3 to 5 minutes. Add the onion to the potato and broth mixture. Transfer the mixture to a food processor or blender, and process until smooth, in batches if necessary. Return to the pot, and stir in 1 cup of the remaining broth, the milk, hot sauce, salt, and pepper. Add more broth if necessary. Cook over low heat for 10 minutes. Sprinkle with green onions, and serve.

Nutritional Information per Serving
Calories 144, Protein (g) 6, Carbohydrate (g) 26, Fat (g) 2,
Calories from Fat (%) 10, Saturated Fat (g) 0,
Dietary Fiber (g) 2, Cholesterol (mg) 1, Sodium (mg) 388
Diabetic Exchanges: 1.5 starch, 1 vegetable

Terrific Tip
TO THICKEN POTATO SOUP, ADD MASHED POTATO FLAKES, 1 TABLESPOON AT A TIME, UNTIL THE SOUP IS THE DESIRED CONSISTENCY.

Terrific Tip
KEEP THE SOUPS ON THE STOVE AND PLACE A BASKET OF SLICED BREAD CLOSE BY SO THAT YOUR GUESTS CAN SERVE THEMSELVES. IT'S CONVENIENT FOR THEM AND EASY ON YOU!

Chicken and Sun-dried Tomato Chili

This recipe works wonderfully with leftover chicken, store-bought rotisserie chicken, or even leftover smoked turkey. Just add the chicken (or turkey) when you add the corn. This easy, packed-with-flavor recipe will quickly become one of your favorites. Serve the avocado and sunflower seeds in condiment bowls to give this white chili a terrific twist.

MAKES 8 SERVINGS

2/3 cup sun-dried tomatoes (not oil-packed)
1/2 cup red wine
1 1/2 pounds boneless, skinless chicken breasts, cut into pieces
3 cups chopped tomatoes
1 (4-ounce) can chopped green chiles
4 cups canned chicken broth
2 tablespoons chili powder
2 cups frozen corn
1 avocado, chopped
2 tablespoons sunflower seeds

In a small bowl, combine the sun-dried tomatoes and red wine, and let stand for 5 minutes to allow the tomatoes to soften.

Coat a large pot with nonstick cooking spray, and set over medium-high heat. Add the chicken to the pot and cook, stirring, until browned, about 5 minutes. Add the chopped tomatoes, and cook, stirring, until tender, 3 to 5 minutes. Add the sun-dried tomato and red wine mixture, the green chiles, chicken broth, and chili powder, and bring to a boil. Add the corn, and cook until the chicken is tender, 7 to 10 minutes. To serve, top with the chopped avocado and sunflower seeds.

Nutritional Information per Serving
Calories 241, Protein (g) 25, Carbohydrate (g) 19, Fat (g) 7, Calories from Fat (%) 25, Saturated Fat (g) 1, Dietary Fiber (g) 5, Cholesterol (mg) 49, Sodium (mg) 364
Diabetic Exchanges: *2.5 lean meat, 0.5 starch, 2 vegetable*

Overnight Layered Salad

This is the perfect make-ahead salad, chock full of wonderful ingredients and topped with a light, creamy Dijon dressing. This salad is best when made the night before and then conveniently pulled out when ready to serve. You may make it just a couple of hours ahead of time, though, if your schedule doesn't permit the overnight interim.

MAKES 10 TO 12 SERVINGS

6 to 8 cups torn salad greens
  (including 1 cup baby spinach, if desired)
1/2 cup shredded carrots
1/2 cup chopped red onion
1 cup frozen peas, thawed
1 cup cherry tomato halves
2 ounces prosciutto, chopped
1/2 cup shredded part-skim mozzarella cheese
3/4 cup buttermilk
3/4 cup fat-free sour cream
2 teaspoons Dijon mustard
1/2 teaspoon dried basil leaves
1/2 teaspoon salt
1/2 teaspoon pepper

In a 3-quart oblong casserole dish, layer the greens, carrots, red onion, peas, tomato halves, prosciutto, and mozzarella. In a medium bowl, mix together the buttermilk, sour cream, Dijon mustard, basil, salt, and pepper, blending well with a fork. Carefully spread the dressing over the salad, spreading to cover. Do not toss. Cover with plastic wrap and refrigerate for at least 2 hours to blend flavors before serving.

Nutritional Information per Serving
Calories 71, Protein (g) 5, Carbohydrate (g) 9, Fat (g) 2, Calories from Fat (%) 22, Saturated Fat (g) 1, Dietary Fiber (g) 2, Cholesterol (mg) 10, Sodium (mg) 276
Diabetic Exchanges: *0.5 lean meat, 0.5 starch*

> ## Terrific Tip
> SELECT SALAD GREENS WITH A VIBRANT GREEN COLOR; THE MORE VIBRANT THE COLOR, THE MORE NUTRITIOUS THE LETTUCE. INCLUDE BABY SPINACH LEAVES FOR ADDED NUTRITION.

Chocolate Loaded Squares

Every bite has the wonderful taste of coconut and pecans, enhanced by mouthfuls of cream cheese filling.

MAKES 28 TO 35 SQUARES

1 (18.25-ounce) box devil's food cake mix
1 egg
4 egg whites, divided
2 tablespoons canola oil
1 1/3 cups water
1/2 cup flaked coconut
1/2 cup chopped pecans
1 (8-ounce) package reduced-fat cream
  cheese, softened
1 1/2 cups confectioners' sugar
1 teaspoon vanilla extract

Preheat the oven to 350°F. Coat a 13 x 9 x 2-inch baking pan with nonstick cooking spray.

Prepare the cake mix with 1 egg, 3 of the egg whites, the canola oil, and water, mixing according to the package directions. Sprinkle the coconut and pecans on the bottom of the prepared baking pan. Carefully pour the chocolate batter on top of the coconut mixture.

In a mixing bowl, beat together the cream cheese, remaining egg white, confectioners' sugar, and vanilla until creamy. Drop by large spoonfuls on top of the chocolate batter—do not stir. Bake for 30 to 35 minutes, or until an inserted toothpick comes out clean.

Nutritional Information per Serving (per sqaure)
Calories 126, Protein (g) 2, Carbohydrate (g) 17, Fat (g) 5, Calories from Fat (%) 38, Saturated Fat (g) 2, Dietary Fiber (g) 1, Cholesterol (mg) 11, Sodium (mg) 152
Diabetic Exchanges: *1 other carbohydrate, 1 fat*

Mardi Gras Madness

The tradition of colorful beads and elaborate parades now stretches from New Orleans, Louisiana, to all across the country. Mardi Gras is one of the fastest growing celebrations in the world and a great excuse to enjoy Cajun flavors. Ingredients such as shrimp, bread pudding, and Louisiana yams are all representative of this unique cuisine. Everyone assumes that Louisiana food is hot and spicy, but I prefer to call it "well seasoned."

Among the menu selections, I have included a festive salad packed with Mardi Gras colors and wonderful flavors. Barbecue Shrimp is high on my list of best-loved recipes, so I recommend preparing it year round. It's a messy dish, yes, but you will not want to leave one ounce of its incredible sauce on your plate. And what better use of old French bread than Bananas Foster Bread Pudding, a New Orleans favorite? All of the recipes are so full of flavor and yet so easy to prepare. A purchased king cake also makes a festive addition to your menu (I like to send them all over the country as gifts)—just remember, whoever finds the baby hidden inside is responsible for buying the next cake!

Mardi Gras is about having a good time, so start the music, toss the beads, and enjoy the food. As they say in New Orleans, "Throw me a party, mister!"

MENU SELECTIONS

EXCITING EXTRAS

- Use traditional Mardi Gras decorations such as colorful beads and festive masks to adorn your table.
- Accent your décor with the Mardi Gras colors of green, purple, and gold.
- Play jazz as background music.
- Order a king cake (see Terrific Tip) to add an extra Mardi Gras feel to your menu.

Terrific Tip

A KING CAKE IS A LARGE, BRIOCHE-TYPE CAKE, SHAPED LIKE A THICK OVAL CROWN AND DECORATED USING THE CARNIVAL COLORS OF GREEN, PURPLE, AND GOLD. IT IS SOLD IN BAKERIES FOR THE PERIOD BETWEEN TWELFTH NIGHT (JANUARY 6) AND ASH WEDNESDAY. AS TRADITION GOES, A TINY CHINA BABY DOLL IS BAKED INTO IT, AND THE PERSON WHO GETS THE SLICE CONTAINING THE DOLL IS OBLIGATED TO BRING THE KING CAKE NEXT TIME.

Short Cuts

▸ Use a store-bought gumbo mix or frozen gumbo as a quick source of Mardi Gras flavor.

▸ Buy an assortment of green, purple, and gold paper napkins to enhance your theme and ensure easy clean-up.

▸ Purchase a loaf of French bread at your local supermarket or bakery to serve fresh.

Louisiana Vegetable Soup

This is a fun, richly flavored soup with a spectrum of color and flavor to match. Occasionally I'll toss in some claw crabmeat or shrimp for a seafood version. I always make an extra batch of this amazing soup to store in the freezer.

MAKES 12 SERVINGS

1 onion, chopped
1 green bell pepper, cored and chopped
1 teaspoon minced garlic
4 cups canned vegetable broth
  or chicken broth
3 cups diced peeled sweet potatoes (yams)
1 (16-ounce) bag frozen corn
2 (14³/4-ounce) cans cream style corn
1 (10-ounce) can chopped tomatoes
  and green chiles
1 (6-ounce) can tomato paste
1 tablespoon Worcestershire sauce
Salt and pepper, to taste
Dash hot pepper sauce
Sliced green onions (scallions), optional

Coat a large pot with nonstick cooking spray, and set over medium heat. Add the onion, bell pepper, and garlic, and cook, stirring, until tender, 3 to 5 minutes. Add the broth, sweet potatoes, frozen corn, cream style corn, tomatoes and green chiles, tomato paste, Worcestershire sauce, salt, pepper, and hot sauce, and bring to a boil. Reduce the heat, and cook until the sweet potatoes are tender, 15 to 20 minutes. Add the green onions, if desired, and add more broth if soup is too thick.

Nutritional Information per Serving
Calories 150, Protein (g) 4, Carbohydrate (g) 36, Fat (g) 1, Calories from Fat (%) 6, Saturated Fat (g) 0, Dietary Fiber (g) 4, Cholesterol (mg) 0, Sodium (mg) 657
Diabetic Exchanges: *2 starch, 1 vegetable*

Terrific Tip
SWEET POTATOES (OR YAMS) HAVE BEEN TOUTED AS ONE OF THE MOST NUTRITIOUS VEGETABLES YOU CAN INCLUDE ON YOUR MENU. FRESH SWEET POTATOES ARE AVAILABLE YEAR ROUND.

Mardi Gras Salad

Get in the spirit with this festive salad of oranges, carrots, bacon, red onions, and green spinach, representing the Mardi Gras colors. Make the delicious, slightly sweet dressing ahead of time, and have the salad ingredients ready to mix together and toss with the dressing when ready to serve.

MAKES 8 TO 10 SERVINGS

2 teaspoons finely chopped onion
1/2 cup cider vinegar
1/4 cup sugar
1/4 cup olive oil
1 teaspoon ground dry mustard
1 head red tip lettuce, washed, drained,
  and torn into pieces
1 (10-ounce) package baby spinach,
  washed and drained
1/2 cup chopped red onion
2 (11-ounce) cans mandarin oranges,
  drained
1/3 cup shredded carrots
4 slices center cut bacon, crisply fried
  and crumbled

In a small bowl, whisk together the onion, vinegar, sugar, olive oil, and mustard. Refrigerate until ready to toss the salad. In a large salad bowl, combine the lettuce, spinach, red onion, mandarin oranges, carrots, and bacon. Toss the salad with the dressing when ready to serve.

Nutritional Information per Serving
Calories 112, Protein (g) 2, Carbohydrate (g) 13, Fat (g) 7, Calories from Fat (%) 50, Saturated Fat (g) 1, Dietary Fiber (g) 2, Cholesterol (mg) 2, Sodium (mg) 78
Diabetic Exchanges: *1 fruit, 1.5 fat*

Terrific Tip
FOR CRISPINESS WITHOUT THE FAT, COOK THE BACON IN THE MICROWAVE AND THEN DRAIN ON PAPER TOWELS. I LIKE TO USE LEANER CENTER CUT BACON WHEN POSSIBLE.

MARDI GRAS SALAD

Garlic Angel Hair

This simple side is great on its own and makes an excellent partner to the Barbecue Shrimp (see page 109).
The sauce of the shrimp mixes with the pasta, making a combination that's hard to beat. I prefer freshly cracked pepper with this recipe.

MAKES 8 TO 10 SERVINGS

1 (16-ounce) package angel hair
  pasta (capellini)
¼ cup olive oil
¼ cup chopped fresh parsley
1 tablespoon minced garlic
Salt and pepper, to taste

Cook the pasta according to the package directions, drain, and set aside. In a small skillet over low heat, add the olive oil, parsley, and garlic, and cook, stirring, for several minutes. Toss with the pasta, and season with salt and pepper.

Nutritional Information per Serving
Calories 218, Protein (g) 6, Carbohydrate (g) 34, Fat (g) 6,
Calories from Fat (%) 26, Saturated Fat (g) 1,
Dietary Fiber (g) 1, Cholesterol (mg) 0, Sodium (mg) 4
Diabetic Exchanges: *2.5 starch, 1 fat*

Terrific Tip
TO MAKE PASTA AHEAD OF TIME AND PREVENT IT FROM STICKING TOGETHER, COOK UNTIL AL DENTE, COAT THE PASTA WITH A LITTLE OLIVE OIL, AND REFRIGERATE IN ZIPPER-TOP PLASTIC BAGS. THEN REHEAT IN THE MICROWAVE OVEN BEFORE USING IN THE RECIPE.

Mozzarella and Onion Stuffed Bread

Every bite of this luscious bread is filled with an onion-cheese mixture that melts in your mouth.
It literally takes just minutes to prepare and will disappear even quicker.

MAKES 12 TO 16 SLICES

1 (16-ounce) loaf Italian bread or
French bread
6 tablespoons (¾ stick) margarine
½ cup finely chopped onion
2 teaspoons Dijon mustard
1 teaspoon poppy seeds
Dash hot pepper sauce
1 cup shredded part-skim mozzarella cheese

Preheat the oven to 350°F. Slice the bread diagonally, taking care not to cut through the bottom crust.

Melt the margarine in a pot over medium heat, add the onion, and cook, stirring, until tender, about 5 minutes. Remove from the heat, and add the mustard, poppy seeds, and hot sauce. Spoon the mixture between the slices of bread. Sprinkle cheese between each slice and a little on top. Transfer the bread to a baking sheet, and bake for 10 to 15 minutes, or until the cheese is melted and the bread is crispy.

Nutritional Information per Serving (per slice)
Calories 136, Protein (g) 4, Carbohydrate (g) 15, Fat (g) 6, Calories from Fat (%) 43,
Saturated Fat (g) 2, Dietary Fiber (g) 1, Cholesterol (mg) 4, Sodium (mg) 264
Diabetic Exchanges: *1 starch, 1 fat*

BARBECUE SHRIMP

Barbecue Shrimp

This fabulous shrimp recipe is an all-time favorite at my house, and dipping chunks of French bread in the sauce is as good as it gets. Messy yet fun to eat, this dish is full of Louisiana tradition—just have plenty of paper towels on hand! I promise this is a five-star recipe that you will make over and over again.

MAKES 4 TO 6 SERVINGS

¼ cup olive oil

2 tablespoons margarine

¼ cup Worcestershire sauce

3 tablespoons lemon juice

1 tablespoon minced garlic

1 tablespoon paprika

2 bay leaves

1 teaspoon dried rosemary leaves

1 teaspoon dried oregano leaves

1 teaspoon dried basil leaves

1 tablespoon hot pepper sauce

Salt and pepper, to taste

2 pounds unpeeled large shrimp

¼ cup white wine

In a large, heavy skillet, combine the olive oil, margarine, Worcestershire sauce, lemon juice, garlic, paprika, bay leaves, rosemary, oregano, basil, hot sauce, salt, and pepper. Cook over medium heat until the sauce begins to boil. Add the shrimp, and cook for about 5 minutes. Add the wine, and cook until the shrimp are done, another 5 to 7 minutes. Serve the shrimp with the sauce.

Nutritional Information per Serving
Calories 251, Protein (g) 24, Carbohydrate (g) 4, Fat (g) 14, Calories from Fat (%) 51, Saturated Fat (g) 2, Dietary Fiber (g) 0, Cholesterol (mg) 224, Sodium (mg) 430
Diabetic Exchanges: *3.5 very lean meat, 2 fat*

Terrific Tip
IF DESIRED, THE SHRIMP MAY BE PEELED BEFORE COOKING IN THE SAUCE FOR EASIER EATING—BUT IT IS JUST NOT THE SAME EXPERIENCE!

CHICKEN AND SAUSAGE JAMBALAYA

Chicken and Sausage Jambalaya

Of course, the best jambalaya is prepared in huge, black, cast iron pots, but this is a quick home version that is equally good. I use chicken and sausage, but feel free to add pork or ham if you prefer. This Louisiana favorite is perfect for a large crowd and makes a great one-dish family meal.

MAKES 6 TO 8 SERVINGS

2 pounds boneless, skinless chicken breasts, cut into small pieces

14 ounces reduced-fat smoked sausage, sliced ½-inch thick

2 cups chopped onion

1 green bell pepper, cored and chopped

1 tablespoon minced garlic

3 cups canned beef broth

1½ cups rice

½ teaspoon chili powder

¼ teaspoon dried thyme leaves

⅛ teaspoon cayenne

Salt and pepper, to taste

1 bunch green onions (scallions), sliced

Coat a large pot with nonstick cooking spray, and set over medium heat. Add the chicken and cook, turning constantly, until browned all over. Remove, and set aside. Coat the same pot again with nonstick cooking spray, and set over medium heat. Add the sausage, and cook, stirring, until lightly browned. Remove, and set aside.

Coat the same pot with nonstick cooking spray, and set over medium heat. Add the onion, bell pepper, and garlic, and cook, stirring, until tender, 5 to 7 minutes, scraping the brown bits from the bottom of the pan—this adds color to the jambalaya. Add the broth, rice, chili powder, thyme, cayenne, salt, pepper, and browned chicken and sausage, and bring to a boil. Lower the heat, cover, and simmer until the liquid is absorbed and the rice is tender, 25 to 30 minutes. Uncover, stir in the green onions, and continue cooking over medium heat for 5 minutes more.

Nutritional Information per Serving
Calories 346, Protein (g) 37, Carbohydrate (g) 39, Fat (g) 3, Calories from Fat (%) 8, Saturated Fat (g) 1, Dietary Fiber (g) 2, Cholesterol (mg) 83, Sodium (mg) 880
Diabetic Exchanges: *4 very lean meat, 2 starch, 2 vegetable*

Bananas Foster Bread Pudding

In this recipe, traditional bread pudding pairs up with the popular New Orleans dessert called Bananas Foster for an irresistible banana sensation. I like to use the cinnamon swirl raisin bread for extra spice. The Bananas Foster Sauce may also be used over vanilla ice cream (nonfat, of course) for another fabulous dessert idea.

MAKES 10 TO 12 SERVINGS

1 (16-ounce) loaf cinnamon-raisin bread, slices cut in fourths
2 tablespoons margarine
3 large bananas, thinly sliced
6 tablespoons sugar, divided
3 eggs
2 egg whites
1 (12-ounce) can fat-free evaporated milk
2 cups fat-free half & half
1 tablespoon vanilla extract
1/2 teaspoon ground cinnamon
1/4 cup chopped pecans, toasted
  (see Terrific Tip, page 22), optional
Bananas Foster Sauce (recipe follows)

BANANAS FOSTER SAUCE:
2 tablespoons margarine
1 1/2 cups dark brown sugar
1/4 cup banana liqueur
2 large bananas, sliced in rounds

Preheat the oven to 350°F. Coat a 3-quart oblong baking dish with nonstick cooking spray. Place the cinnamon-raisin bread pieces the bottom of the baking dish.

In a medium skillet over medium heat, melt the margarine. Add the bananas and 2 tablespoon of the sugar, and cook until the bananas are tender, about 3 minutes. Remove from the heat, and add the bananas to the bread mixture, mixing slightly.

In a mixing bowl, blend together the remaining 4 tablespoons of sugar, the eggs, egg whites, evaporated milk, half & half, vanilla, and cinnamon, mixing with a whisk. Carefully pour over the banana-bread mixture, and press gently to compact. Let sit for about 10 minutes. Bake for 40 to 50 minutes, or until set and the top is golden brown. If desired, top with toasted pecans. Serve immediately with the Bananas Foster Sauce.

Bananas Foster Sauce: In a large skillet over medium heat, melt the margarine, and mix in the brown sugar to form a creamy paste. Add the liqueur and banana slices, and cook over low heat until the bananas are tender but not mushy, 3 to 5 minutes.

Nutritional Information per Serving
Calories 376, Protein (g) 11, Carbohydrate (g) 72, Fat (g) 6, Calories from Fat (%) 13, Saturated Fat (g) 1, Dietary Fiber (g) 3, Cholesterol (mg) 54, Sodium (mg) 231
Diabetic Exchanges: *1 very lean meat, 1 fruit, 4 other carbohydrate, 1 fat*

Terrific Tip
BECAUSE OF THE HIGH SUGAR CONTENT, DIABETICS MAY NEED TO LIMIT THEMSELVES TO A SMALLER PORTION, BUT IT IS WORTH EVERY BITE.

Mardi Gras Punch

Get in the spirit of Mardi Gras with this purplish punch, full of wonderful juices. Slice limes to float on top. To serve a smaller group, you can easily halve the ingredients, or just store any extra in the refrigerator for a great fruit drink anytime.

MAKES ABOUT 24 (8-OUNCE) SERVINGS

3 cups grape juice
1 (46-ounce) can pineapple juice
4 cups orange juice
1 (2-liter) bottle ginger ale
Limes, sliced

In a large bowl or container, mix together the grape juice, pineapple juice, and orange juice. Pour in the ginger ale before serving. Garnish with limes.

Nutritional Information per Serving
Calories 75, Protein (g) 0, Carbohydrate (g) 19, Fat (g) 0, Calories from Fat (%) 0, Saturated Fat (g) 0, Dietary Fiber (g) 0, Cholesterol (mg) 0, Sodium (mg) 6
Diabetic Exchanges: *1 fruit*

Terrific Tip

BEFORE MAKING THE PUNCH, PLACE THE BOTTLE OF GINGER ALE IN THE FREEZER UNTIL IT BECOMES ICY. JUST DON'T FORGET AND LEAVE IT THERE!

Orient Express

When you crave Chinese food, your first inclination may be to order takeout from a local restaurant. However, nowadays, Asian cuisine has mainstreamed its way into most home kitchens. With the exotic spices and sauces that entice our taste buds now readily available in local supermarkets, experiencing the Far East is as easy as a dinner at home. A stir-fry is the perfect choice for a quick meal, and the Lettuce Wraps are great fun to both prepare and eat. Chinese food effortlessly serves a crowd, making it perfect for large, casual gatherings. I've fed a house full of teenagers and prepared fun family dinners by offering a selection of Asian dishes. Sometimes we even pick up sushi from one of our favorite shop or restaurant, as I don't like to spend the extra time making it when you can purchase it so easily. Absolute must-have condiments include soy sauce and wasabi. And don't let chopsticks intimidate you—I myself have not mastered the skill of using them, but they are great for setting the mood. The Orient Express menu represents some of my favorite recipes, but don't hesitate to supplement it with your personal favorites or selections from your restaurant of choice.

MENU SELECTIONS

EXCITING EXTRAS

▶ Offer chopsticks for a more authentic eating experience.

▶ Have small bowls readily available for soy sauce, wasabi, and sweet-and-sour sauce.

▶ Set your table with bamboo place mats.

▶ Use Asian-style serving platters, which can often be found in variety stores, to set the mood.

▶ Choose orchids, tiger lilies, or stems of ginger flowers (ask your florist if they can get this) when creating floral decorations.

Short Cuts

▶ Supplement your menu with takeout from your favorite Chinese restaurant.

▶ Pick up sushi and fortune cookies.

▶ Make Chinese Chocolate Noodle Drops ahead of time, and refrigerate until ready to serve.

Asian Caesar Salad with Seasoned Won Tons

The Asian influence on the classic Caesar salad adds the perfect touch to this menu. After trying this recipe, you will want to make extra won tons for snacks. If you have black sesame seeds in your pantry, sprinkle about 1 teaspoon on the salad for extra flair and flavor. The crisp, seasoned won tons are my Asian version of croutons. Won ton wrappers are usually sold in the refrigerated produce section of the supermarket, alongside other Asian ingredients like fresh noodles and tofu.

MAKES 6 SERVINGS

1 large head romaine lettuce, washed
  and torn into pieces
2 tablespoons grated Parmesan cheese
2 tablespoons lemon juice
1 tablespoon reduced-sodium soy sauce
1/2 teaspoon sesame oil
1/4 teaspoon garlic powder
Dash hot pepper sauce
1/3 cup nonfat sour cream
Seasoned Won Tons (recipe follows)

SEASONED WON TONS:
1 tablespoon sesame seeds
1/2 teaspoon garlic powder
1/2 teaspoon paprika
1/4 teaspoon salt
12 won ton wrappers, cut in half
  diagonally to form triangles

In a large bowl, combine the lettuce and Parmesan cheese. In a small bowl, combine the lemon juice, soy sauce, sesame oil, garlic powder, and hot sauce. Stir in the sour cream. Add the dressing mixture to the lettuce, tossing to coat well. Arrange on salad plates and top each serving with 4 Seasoned Won Tons.

Seasoned Won Tons: Preheat the oven to 375°F. Coat a baking sheet with nonstick cooking spray.
  In a small bowl, combine the sesame seeds, garlic powder, paprika, and salt. Place the won ton triangles on the prepared baking sheet. Coat each wrapper with nonstick cooking spray, or brush with olive oil. Sprinkle the seasoning mixture evenly over the won ton triangles. Bake for 4 to 5 minutes, or until crisp and golden brown. Cool and store in an airtight container until ready to serve.

Nutritional Information per Serving
Calories 105, Protein (g) 6, Carbohydrate (g) 16, Fat (g) 2, Calories from Fat (%) 19, Saturated Fat (g) 1, Dietary Fiber (g) 3, Cholesterol (mg) 5, Sodium (mg) 225
Diabetic Exchanges: *1 starch, 0.5 fat*

Terrific Tip
WON TON PATTY SHELLS ARE PERFECT FOR SERVING WITH HOT DIPS. PLACE A WON TON WRAPPER IN EACH TIN OF A MINI MUFFIN PAN COATED WITH NONSTICK COOKING SPRAY, AND BAKE IN A PREHEATED 350°F OVEN FOR 10 MINUTES, OR UNTIL LIGHT BROWN. COOL, AND STORE IN ZIPPER-TOP PLASTIC BAGS.

Vegetable Fried Rice

Fried rice makes a great side dish or light meal. This simple, satisfying recipe can be made ahead of time, freeing you to concentrate on the other components of a larger meal.

MAKES 4 TO 6 SERVINGS

1/4 cup reduced-sodium soy sauce

1 tablespoon lemon juice

1 tablespoon light brown sugar

1 teaspoon minced garlic

1 teaspoon ground ginger

1/4 teaspoon crushed red pepper flakes, optional

1 tablespoon olive oil

1 1/2 cups fresh broccoli florets

1 cup sliced fresh mushrooms

1/2 cup chopped onion

1/2 cup thinly sliced carrot sticks

4 cups cooked white rice

2 eggs, lightly beaten and cooked, cut into strips

1 bunch green onions (scallions), sliced

In a small bowl, mix together the soy sauce, lemon juice, brown sugar, garlic, ginger, and red pepper flakes, if desired, and set aside.

In a large skillet over medium-high heat, add the oil, broccoli, mushrooms, onion, and carrot sticks, and cook, stirring, for 3 minutes. Add the soy sauce mixture to the skillet, and stir to combine. Continue cooking until the vegetables are crisp tender, 5 to 7 minutes. Add the rice, eggs, and green onions, tossing until everything is well heated.

Nutritional Information per Serving
Calories 221, Protein (g) 7, Carbohydrate (g) 38, Fat (g) 4, Calories from Fat (%) 18, Saturated Fat (g) 1, Dietary Fiber (g) 2, Cholesterol (mg) 71, Sodium (mg) 295
Diabetic Exchanges: *2 starch, 1.5 vegetable, 0.5 fat*

Terrific Tip
FOR A HEARTIER, FULLY-LOADED FRIED RICE DISH, I ADD PIECES OF COOKED PORK, CHICKEN, OR SHRIMP WITH THE VEGGIES. THIS IS A CLEGG FAMILY SPECIALTY!

Terrific Tip

BUY SUSHI FROM YOUR FAVORITE SHOP
OR RESTAURANT TO ADD TO YOUR MENU.

Glazed Shrimp with Broccoli and Snow Peas

*Even though this stir-fry can be made in just minutes, it boasts flavor, texture, and color that will please
the simple to the sophisticated palate.*

MAKES 4 SERVINGS

1 cup canned chicken broth
2 tablespoons hoisin sauce
1 tablespoon cornstarch
1 teaspoon ground ginger
1 tablespoon olive oil
1 red bell pepper, cored and chopped
1 teaspoon minced garlic
2 cups broccoli florets
1 1/2 pounds medium shrimp, peeled
1 (6-ounce) package frozen snow peas
4 green onions (scallions), sliced
2 teaspoons sesame seeds, toasted

In a small bowl, combine the chicken broth, hoisin sauce, cornstarch, and ginger, and set
aside. In a large skillet over medium-high heat, heat the olive oil. Add the bell pepper and
garlic, and cook, stirring, until tender, 3 to 5 minutes. Add the broccoli, shrimp, snow peas,
and hoisin mixture, and mix well. Bring to a boil, and cook over medium-high heat until
the shrimp are done and the vegetables are crisp tender, about 5 minutes. Sprinkle with the
green onions and sesame seeds, and serve immediately.

Nutritional Information per Serving
*Calories 234, Protein (g) 31, Carbohydrate (g) 13,
Fat (g) 6, Calories from Fat (%) 23,
Saturated Fat (g) 1, Dietary Fiber (g) 3,
Cholesterol (mg) 252, Sodium (mg) 458*
Diabetic Exchanges: *4 lean meat, 3 vegetable*

Terrific Tip

TO TOAST SESAME SEEDS, BAKE IN A SMALL BAKING PAN
IN A PREHEATED 350°F OVEN FOR ABOUT 5 MINUTES, OR
UNTIL LIGHT GOLDEN BROWN. WATCH CAREFULLY TO AVOID
BURNING. TOASTED SESAME SEEDS ARE ALSO NOW SOLD IN
JARS IN THE ASIAN SECTION OR THE SPICE SECTION OF
MANY SUPERMARKETS.

Terrific Tip

IF RED BELL PEPPERS ARE NOT AVAILABLE OR
TOO COSTLY, SUBSTITUTE GREEN BELL PEPPERS.

Lettuce Wraps with Homemade Hoisin Sauce

This easy, home version of Lettuce Wraps combines amazing ingredients for the perfect wrap. I prefer letting everyone make their own wraps instead of serving them already prepared—they are as fun to make as they are to eat. For quick preparation, I put the mushrooms, carrots, chicken, water chestnuts, and bamboo shoots in the food processor, and chop everything finely all at once. The Homemade Hoisin Sauce is absolutely delicious, so be sure to make plenty!

MAKES 4 TO 6 SERVINGS

1 cup finely chopped fresh mushrooms

1/2 cup finely chopped carrots

3 cups finely diced cooked chicken

1 (8-ounce) can water chestnuts, drained and finely chopped

1 (8-ounce) can bamboo shoots, drained and finely chopped

1/2 cup sliced green onions (scallions)

1/2 cup frozen peas, thawed

1 tablespoon oyster sauce

1 teaspoon sugar

1 teaspoon reduced-sodium soy sauce

1/2 teaspoon sesame oil

1 bunch red tip or butter leaf lettuce, washed and dried

Homemade Hoisin Sauce (recipe follows), for dipping

Coat a skillet with nonstick cooking spray, and set over medium-high heat. Cook the mushrooms and carrots, stirring, until tender, about 3 minutes. Add the chicken, water chestnuts, and bamboo shoots, stirring until heated through. Remove from the heat, and mix in the green onions and peas.

In a small bowl, mix together the oyster sauce, sugar, soy sauce, and sesame oil. Add the sauce mixture to the chicken mixture, mixing well.

To serve, take a large lettuce leaf, top with some of the chicken mixture, and wrap the lettuce leaf around. Serve with the Homemade Hoisin Sauce.

Nutritional Information per Serving (without Homemade Hoisin Sauce)
Calories 166, Protein (g) 20, Carbohydrate (g) 9, Fat (g) 5, Calories from Fat (%) 29, Saturated Fat (g) 1, Dietary Fiber (g) 3, Cholesterol (mg) 53, Sodium (mg) 211
Diabetic Exchanges: *2.5 lean meat, 2 vegetable*

Homemade Hoisin Sauce

Of course, hoisin sauce can be purchased at the store, but this recipe is so simple and the result is far better than any sauce in a jar. It couldn't be easier to double or even triple this tasty recipe, and you'll want to once you see how much everyone enjoys it! Serve in a bowl to accompany the Lettuce Wraps.

MAKES 6 (2-TABLESPOON) SERVINGS

6 teaspoons sugar

6 tablespoons oyster sauce

6 teaspoons reduced-sodium soy sauce

3 teaspoons sesame oil

Mix together the sugar, oyster sauce, soy sauce, and sesame oil to make sauce. Use this amount as the basic recipe and times it for as much sauce as desired.

Nutritional Information per Serving
Calories 58, Protein (g) 2, Carbohydrate (g) 7, Fat (g) 2, Calories from Fat (%) 36, Saturated Fat (g) 0, Dietary Fiber (g) 0, Cholesterol (mg) 0, Sodium (mg) 802
Diabetic Exchanges: *0.5 other carbohydrate, 0.5 fat*

Chinese Chocolate Noodle Drops

As my daughter Haley says, once you eat one of these drops, you just can't stop! Chocolate, peanuts, and peanut butter team up with Chinese noodles to make this easy-to-make, easy-to-eat dessert an official Asian treat. Chow mein noodles are available in the Asian aisle at most supermarkets.

MAKES 40 TO 48 DROPS

1¼ cups sugar
6 tablespoons (¾ stick) margarine
½ cup skim milk
¼ cup cocoa
½ cup reduced-fat peanut butter
1 teaspoon vanilla extract
3 cups chow mein noodles
½ cup peanut halves

In a large saucepan over medium heat, stir together the sugar, margarine, milk, and cocoa until dissolved. Bring the mixture to a boil, and boil for 2 minutes. Remove from the heat. Mix in the peanut butter and vanilla. Beat by hand until thickened. Carefully stir in the chow mein noodles and peanuts. Drop by teaspoonfuls onto waxed paper. Refrigerate until firm, and store in a cool place or the refrigerator.

Nutritional Information per Serving (per drop)
Calories 73, Protein (g) 2, Carbohydrate (g) 8, Fat (g) 4, Calories from Fat (%) 47, Saturated Fat (g) 1, Dietary Fiber (g) 0, Cholesterol (mg) 0, Sodium (mg) 45
Diabetic Exchanges: *0.5 other carbohydrate, 1 fat*

Comfort Sundays

Lounging in the well-worn recliner, reading each section of the newspaper, and flicking through the television channels sums up what I call a Comfort Sunday. On such days, it seems there is more time available for cooking, and it's easier for everyone to get together to eat. Today, comfort food has become a defined cuisine in itself, but I still consider it to be just a wide array of traditional recipes that have been in my kitchen for years. Classic dishes like meatloaf, broccoli, potatoes, and cake are still on this menu but with an updated makeover. Roasted Fanned Potatoes, wonderfully browned and full of flavor, are simple to prepare and will be the talk of the meal. Carrot Pudding makes eating veggies a heavenly delight, and nothing ends a meal better than a slice of Apricot and Almond Toffee Cake. After a filling meal of all of my old favorites, I'm always glad that it's Sunday and I get to just relax and digest!

MENU SELECTIONS

EXCITING EXTRAS

▶ Pick up a bunch of flowers at the supermarket for a nice and easy table decoration.

▶ Serve drinks with simple but decorative cocktail napkins before dinner.

▶ Create a casual atmosphere by serving your Sunday meal on individual TV trays instead of seating everyone at the table.

▶ Garnish recipes with tomato roses (see Terrific Tip, page 128) or lemon slices for color.

Short Cuts

▸ **Serve baked or mashed potatoes as a simple and traditional side dish.**

▸ **Purchase rolls from you local bakery or supermarket.**

▸ **Instead of slicing vegetables yourself, purchase pre-cut broccoli and cauliflower.**

OLD-FASHIONED MEAT LOAF

Mixed Green Salad
with Toasted Sesame Seeds and Parmesan Cheese

This simple salad accented with Parmesan cheese and toasted sesame seeds has been my family's "quickie" salad for years. I like to use reduced-fat Caesar dressing or combine two dressings, as I suggest in this recipe. Tossing in some seasonal fruit is also nice.

MAKES 6 SERVINGS

8 cups assorted lettuce leaves
¼ cup grated Parmesan cheese
1 tablespoon sesame seeds, toasted
(see Terrific Tip, page 118)
2 tablespoons reduced-fat Ranch Dressing
3 tablespoons fat-free Italian Dressing

In a bowl, mix together the lettuce, Parmesan cheese, and sesame seeds. When ready to serve, mix together the Ranch Dressing and Italian Dressing, and toss with the salad.

Nutritional Information per Serving
Calories 58, Protein (g) 3, Carbohydrate (g) 3, Fat (g) 4,
Calories from Fat (%) 59, Saturated Fat (g) 1,
Dietary Fiber (g) 1, Cholesterol (mg) 5, Sodium (mg) 228
Diabetic Exchanges: *1 vegetable, 1 fat*

Terrific Tip
FOR A DINNER SALAD, YOU'LL NEED APPROXIMATELY 1 CUP (A HANDFUL) OF GREENS PER PERSON.

Old-Fashioned Meat Loaf

Meat loaf always hits the spot, and the barbecue sauce flavor and special topping give this classic some extra personality. This is a timeless, never-out-of-fashion meat dish that every member of my family requests.

MAKES 8 SERVINGS

1½ pounds ground sirloin

⅓ cup barbecue sauce

1 egg white

½ cup Italian bread crumbs

½ cup chopped onion

1 green bell pepper, cored and finely chopped

1 teaspoon minced garlic

Salt and pepper, to taste

½ cup ketchup

2 tablespoons light brown sugar

1 tablespoon Worcestershire sauce

1 teaspoon Dijon mustard

Preheat the oven to 375°F. Coat a 9 x 5 x 3-inch loaf pan with nonstick cooking spray.

In a bowl, combine the sirloin, barbecue sauce, egg white, bread crumbs, onion, green pepper, garlic, salt, and pepper, and mix well. Transfer to the prepared loaf pan. In a small bowl, mix together the ketchup, brown sugar, Worcestershire sauce, and mustard. Spread the sauce on top of the meat mixture. Bake for 1 hour. Drain off any excess grease before serving.

Nutritional Information per Serving
Calories 186, Protein (g) 19, Carbohydrate (g) 19, Fat (g) 4, Calories from Fat (%) 19, Saturated Fat (g) 2, Dietary Fiber (g) 1, Cholesterol (mg) 45, Sodium (mg) 449
Diabetic Exchanges: *2.5 lean meat, 1 starch*

Terrific Tip
FOR AN ADDED TOUCH, MAKE THE MEAT LOAF IN MINI LOAF PANS TO CREATE INDIVIDUAL SERVINGS READY FOR EACH PLATE.

Broccoli and Cauliflower Casserole

Broccoli and cauliflower team up with an appealing, light cheese sauce in this true comfort casserole. Of course, either vegetable may be used by itself, if desired.

MAKES 8 TO 10 SERVINGS

1 bunch broccoli, florets only (about 4 cups)

1 bunch cauliflower, florets only (about 4 cups)

1 tablespoon margarine

1 cup chopped onion

½ teaspoon minced garlic

2 tablespoons all-purpose flour

1⅓ cups skim milk

1 (8-ounce) package reduced-fat cream cheese

3 tablespoons Italian bread crumbs

2 tablespoons grated Parmesan cheese

Fresh parsley

Preheat the oven to 350°F. Coat a 2-quart casserole dish with nonstick cooking spray.

Cook the broccoli and cauliflower in ½ cup of water in a microwaveable dish, covered, until tender, 6 to 8 minutes. Drain well, and set aside. In a medium pot over medium-high heat, melt the margarine. Add the onion and garlic, and cook, stirring, until tender, about 5 minutes. Stir in the flour. Gradually add the milk, stirring until the mixture thickens. Add the cream cheese, and stir until the cheese melts.

Transfer the cooked broccoli and cauliflower to the prepared casserole dish, and carefully combine with the sauce. Mix together the bread crumbs and Parmesan cheese, and sprinkle over the vegetables. Bake for 20 to 30 minutes, or until heated through and bubbly. Sprinkle with parsley, and serve.

Nutritional Information per Serving
Calories 120, Protein (g) 6, Carbohydrate (g) 10, Fat (g) 7, Calories from Fat (%) 47, Saturated Fat (g) 4, Dietary Fiber (g) 2, Cholesterol (mg) 17, Sodium (mg) 197
Diabetic Exchanges: *2 vegetable, 1.5 fat*

GLAZED SALMON, ROASTED BROCCOLI WITH LEMON-GARLIC SAUCE, and ROASTED FANNED POTATOES

Glazed Salmon

Salmon is rich in the right kind of fat, making it a terrific fish choice, and it's great either grilled or pan sautéed.
The easy, make-ahead marinade gives this dish a gourmet appeal. You can also use sea bass for this recipe.

MAKES 6 SERVINGS

¼ cup soy sauce
¼ cup rice wine vinegar
2 tablespoons light brown sugar
1 teaspoon ground dry mustard
1 teaspoon ground ginger
½ teaspoon pepper
6 (6-ounce) salmon fillets

In a small bowl, mix together the soy sauce, vinegar, brown sugar, mustard, ginger, and pepper. Combine the marinade and salmon in an oblong dish and refrigerate, covered, for at least 1 hour, or overnight.

When ready to serve, prepare a medium-hot grill. Grill the fish for 3 to 4 minutes per side, or until done. You may also coat a nonstick skillet with nonstick cooking spray, and cook the salmon over medium-high heat until crispy on the outside and tender inside, 3 to 4 minutes per side. Discard any marinade, and be careful not to overcook the fish.

Nutritional Information per Serving
Calories 226, Protein (g) 38, Carbohydrate (g) 2, Fat (g) 6, Calories from Fat (%) 27,
Saturated Fat (g) 1, Dietary Fiber (g) 0, Cholesterol (mg) 97, Sodium (mg) 385
Diabetic Exchanges: *5 lean meat*

HOLLY CLEGG'S TRIM & TERRIFIC™ HOME ENTERTAINING THE EASY WAY

Roasted Fanned Potatoes

Try this recipe as a nice alternative to the baked potato. I love the crispy outside coating of this simple yet outstanding dish.

MAKES 8 SERVINGS

4 medium Yukon gold potatoes
  or baking potatoes
1/2 cup Italian bread crumbs
1/4 cup grated Parmesan cheese
3 tablespoons olive oil, divided
Paprika

Preheat the oven to 450°F.

Peel the potatoes, and halve lengthwise. Lay the potato halves on a cutting board and cut thin slices in a row, taking care not to cut all the way through to the bottom. Carefully bend to separate each section, not to break potato but to form a potato fan.

In a shallow dish, mix together the bread crumbs, Parmesan cheese, and 1 tablespoon of the olive oil. Drizzle the potatoes with the remaining 2 tablespoons of olive oil, and roll the tops of each potato in the crumb mixture. Sprinkle each potato with paprika. Arrange the potatoes in a baking dish, cover with foil, and bake for 30 minutes. Remove the foil and continue baking for 15 minutes longer, or until the crumbs are browned and the potatoes are cooked.

Nutritional Information per Serving
Calories 134, Protein (g) 4, Carbohydrate (g) 18, Fat (g) 6, Calories from Fat (%) 38,
Saturated Fat (g) 1, Dietary Fiber (g) 2, Cholesterol (mg) 2, Sodium (mg) 154
Diabetic Exchanges: *1 starch, 1 fat*

Vermicelli and Rice

This is one of those very kid-friendly recipes, and, when you add the toasted almonds, it becomes quite impressive to adults, too.

MAKES 6 SERVINGS

1 tablespoon margarine
1 cup rice
1 cup vermicelli pasta, broken into pieces
1 (10.5-ounce) can onion soup
1 1/2 cups water
1/4 cup sliced almonds, toasted
  (see Terrific Tip, page 22), optional

In a medium pot over medium heat, melt the margarine, then add the rice and cook, stirring, for 1 minute. Add the vermicelli, onion soup, and water. Bring to a boil, cover, reduce the heat to low, and simmer until the rice and noodles are done, 20 to 25 minutes. Stir in the almonds, if desired.

Nutritional Information per Serving
Calories 217, Protein (g) 6, Carbohydrate (g) 41, Fat (g) 3, Calories from Fat (%) 13,
Saturated Fat (g) 1, Dietary Fiber (g) 1, Cholesterol (mg) 0, Sodium (mg) 453
Diabetic Exchanges: *2.5 starch*

Roasted Broccoli with Lemon-Garlic Sauce

Try roasting the broccoli with these few ingredients for an intensely flavored, no-fuss veggie.
Top with toasted pecans, walnuts, or pine nuts for that added touch of crunch and pizzazz.

MAKES 8 SERVINGS

3 tablespoons olive oil
1½ teaspoons minced garlic
Salt and pepper, to taste
8 cups broccoli florets
2 tablespoons lemon juice

Preheat the oven to 500°F.

In a large bowl, combine the olive oil, garlic, salt, and pepper. Add the broccoli, and toss to combine. Arrange the broccoli on a baking sheet in a single layer and roast, turning once, for 10 to 15 minutes, or until tender. Remove from the oven, toss with the lemon juice, and serve.

Nutritional Information per Serving
Calories 66, Protein (g) 2, Carbohydrate (g) 4, Fat (g) 5, Calories from Fat (%) 65, Saturated Fat (g) 1, Dietary Fiber (g) 2, Cholesterol (mg) 0, Sodium (mg) 19
Diabetic Exchanges: *1 vegetable, 1 fat*

Quick Cheese Bread

The cheese that oozes from each piece of this wonderful bread keeps everyone grabbing for another piece.
And it starts out with store-bought biscuits—shhhh!

MAKES 6 TO 8 SERVINGS

1 cup shredded reduced-fat sharp Cheddar
 cheese
2 tablespoons skim milk
½ teaspoon ground dry mustard
¼ cup sliced green onions (scallions)
2 (10-count) cans flaky biscuits

Preheat the oven to 375°F. Coat a 9 x 5 x 3-inch loaf pan with nonstick cooking spray.

Combine the Cheddar cheese, milk, mustard, and green onions. Place some of the mixture on top of each biscuit. Arrange the biscuits in two rows with cheese mixture in between in the prepared loaf pan. Bake for 25 to 30 minutes, or until golden brown.

Nutritional Information per Serving
Calories 200, Protein (g) 7, Carbohydrate (g) 22, Fat (g) 10, Calories from Fat (%) 42, Saturated Fat (g) 3, Dietary Fiber (g) 0, Cholesterol (mg) 8, Sodium (mg) 640
Diabetic Exchanges: *0.5 lean meat, 1.5 starch, 1.5 fat*

Carrot Pudding

Here's a wonderful way to sneak carrots in your meal! This slightly sweet pudding entices everyone.

MAKES 8 SERVINGS

2 pounds carrots, peeled and sliced
1/2 cup sugar
1/2 cup all-purpose flour
11/2 teaspoons baking powder
1/2 teaspoon ground cinnamon
2 tablespoons margarine, melted
4 egg whites

Preheat the oven to 350°F. Coat an 11 x 7 x 2-inch baking pan with nonstick cooking spray.

In a pot over medium-high heat, cook the carrots in 1/2 cup of water, covered, until very soft, about 8 minutes, and drain. (You may also cook the carrots in a microwaveable dish in the microwave oven.) Transfer the carrots to a mixer or food processor, and add the sugar, mixing well. In a bowl, mix together the flour, baking powder, and cinnamon, and add to the carrot mixture, along with the melted margarine. In another mixing bowl, beat the egg whites until soft peaks form (see Terrific Tip, page 76). Gradually fold the egg whites into the carrot mixture, mixing just until combined. Transfer to the prepared baking pan, and bake for 40 to 50 minutes, or until browned and set.

Nutritional Information per Serving
Calories 160, Protein (g) 4, Carbohydrate (g) 31, Fat (g) 3, Calories from Fat (%) 17, Saturated Fat (g) 1, Dietary Fiber (g) 4, Cholesterol (mg) 0, Sodium (mg) 192
Diabetic Exchanges: *1 starch, 3 vegetable, 0.5 fat*

Apricot and Almond Toffee Cake

Each bite of this cobbler-type cake simply melts in your mouth.

MAKES 16 SERVINGS

1 (29-ounce) can apricot halves with juice
1 (18.25-ounce) box yellow cake mix
3/4 cup almond toffee bits
1/2 cup flaked coconut
1/3 cup sliced almonds
6 tablespoons (3/4 stick) margarine, melted

Preheat the oven to 350°F. Coat a 13 x 9 x 2-inch baking pan with nonstick cooking spray.

Chop the apricots, and spread the apricots and the canning juice in the prepared pan. Sprinkle the apricots with the yellow cake mix, toffee bits, coconut, and almonds. Drizzle the top with the melted margarine. Do not stir. Bake for 45 minutes to 1 hour, or until the top is crispy. Serve warm or at room temperature.

Nutritional Information per Serving
Calories 279, Protein (g) 2, Carbohydrate (g) 41, Fat (g) 12, Calories from Fat (%) 39, Saturated Fat (g) 3, Dietary Fiber (g) 1, Cholesterol (mg) 4, Sodium (mg) 335
Diabetic Exchanges: *0.5 fruit, 2 other carbohydrate, 2.5 fat*

Classic Cocktail Party

I'm inclined these days to entertain by hosting a cocktail party instead of a formal, sit-down dinner. With the fast pace of life today, a cocktail party gives guests the opportunity to arrive whenever they can, mingle, talk, and sample a variety of recipes. Typically, many people designate the dining room as the place to serve all the food. However, if there is a large crowd, this area often becomes jammed as the guests line up to fill their plates. I have had great success spreading the food throughout my home, taking advantage of coffee tables, end tables, and similar surfaces to promote a flow of people from room to room.

I love cocktail foods, so I have provided quite a selection on this menu. Each and every one of these simple dishes will earn you rave reviews. The tenderloin is a little pricey but your guests will treasure every bite of this seasoned, succulent meat. The Mediterranean Trio offers a trendy assortment of fabulous dips. The Miniature Crab Cakes may be made ahead of time, saving you from stress as you prepare for your company. Brie is a sure success, and the Layered Sun-dried Tomato, Pine Nut and Spinach Spread will grab everyone's attention. It seems that people migrate to the Marinated Shrimp, but the Shrimp Chipotle Cup recipe is an equally delicious and more economical way to include shrimp on your menu. Although there are no desserts listed here, other recipes throughout this book (like the Chocolate Espresso Brownies, page 59, or Lemon Custard Bars, page 32) will satisfy any sweet tooth and make great additions to your cocktail party.

Plates, of course, are a must, but you can probably get away without providing forks as I've aimed to include only finger foods.

MENU SELECTIONS

EXCITING EXTRAS

▶ Decorate the plates with food garnishes such as radish flowers and tomato roses. (See Terrific Tip, page 128)

▶ Use glassware instead of plastic.

▶ Use small skewers or frilled toothpicks to skewer the Sesame Chicken.

▶ To encourage movement and mingling, serve the food in various areas around the house, placing dishes on coffee tables and on the bar as well as on the dining room table. Just make sure to keep the heavier food items on a strong, study surface.

▶ Lay flowers on the tables for a stylish accent.

▶ Decorate with gladiolas in a crystal vase. Gladiolas are tall, impressive flowers that can make quite a statement.

Short Cuts

▶ Use only easy-to-eat
finger foods so no utensils
are needed.

▶ Instead of making scones,
pick up small rolls from
the supermarket or deli
to accompany the Pepper
Dijon Tenderloin.

▶ Use pork tenderloin
in place of the beef
tenderloin—pork is a
less expensive cut.

MEDITERRANEAN SPREAD, HUMMUS and EGGPLANT SPREAD

MEDITERRANEAN TRIO OF TAPENADES

Serve these three Mediterranean recipes together on one large platter for an enticing
Middle Eastern assortment with pita crisps or toasted pita triangles.

Mediterranean Spread

To simplify and speed up the chopping process, chop the artichoke hearts, olives, and onion in the food processor. If desired, the feta cheese may be omitted and served separately as another condiment on the platter. Serve with toasted pita triangles or pita chips.

MAKES 24 (2-TABLESPOON) SERVINGS

1 (14-ounce) can artichoke hearts,
  drained and finely chopped
1 (2¼-ounce) can black olives,
  drained and finely chopped
½ cup pimento-stuffed green olives,
  finely chopped
⅓ cup finely chopped red onion
1 teaspoon minced garlic
⅓ cup crumbled feta cheese
2 tablespoons reduced-fat cream
  cheese, softened

In a large bowl, mix together the artichoke hearts, black olives, green olives, onion, garlic, and feta cheese until well mixed. With a fork, blend in the cream cheese, and serve.

Nutritional Information per Serving
*Calories 20, Protein (g) 1, Carbohydrate (g) 1, Fat (g) 1, Calories from Fat (%) 61,
Saturated Fat (g) 1, Dietary Fiber (g) 0, Cholesterol (mg) 3, Sodium (mg) 167*
Diabetic Exchanges: *Free*

Hummus

This popular Middle Eastern dip is best served with toasted pita triangles. To serve, I suggest shaping the mixture into a mound on a flat plate, then making an indentation in center and filling it with another teaspoon of olive oil

MAKES 24 (2-TABLESPOON) SERVINGS

2 (15-ounce) cans garbanzo beans
  (chickpeas), drained and rinsed
1/2 cup water
2 tablespoons lemon juice
2 tablespoons tahini (sesame paste)
1/2 teaspoon minced garlic
1/2 teaspoon ground cumin
Paprika

Place the garbanzo beans in a food processor or blender, processing until smooth. Add the water, lemon juice, tahini, garlic, and cumin, and process until blended. Sprinkle with paprika before serving.

Nutritional Information per Serving
Calories 41, Protein (g) 2, Carbohydrate (g) 6, Fat (g) 1, Calories from Fat (%) 29, Saturated Fat (g) 0, Dietary Fiber (g) 1, Cholesterol (mg) 0, Sodium (mg) 71
Diabetic Exchanges: *0.5 starch*

Terrific Tip
WHEN DETERMINING HOW MANY GUESTS TO EXPECT, COUNT THE INVITATIONS AND NOT PEOPLE. YOU CAN EXPECT ABOUT FIFTY-FIVE TO SIXTY-FIVE PERCENT OF THOSE INVITED WILL COME.

Eggplant Spread

In Middle Eastern culture, this traditional recipe is referred to as "baba ghanoush." I am partial to eggplant, so here is my personal version. Serve with toasted pita triangles or pita chips.

MAKES 12 (2-TABLESPOON) SERVINGS

1 large eggplant
1 tablespoon minced onion
1 tablespoon olive oil
1 tablespoon tahini (sesame paste)
1 tablespoon lemon juice
1/2 teaspoon minced garlic
Salt
Dash cayenne pepper
Fresh parsley, for garnish

Preheat the oven to 375°F.
  Poke a few holes in the eggplant skin with a sharp knife, wrap it in foil, and roast in the oven for 50 minutes, or until very tender. Cool slightly, cut the eggplant in half lengthwise, and scoop out all of the flesh into a food processor or blender. Add the onion, olive oil, tahini, lemon juice, and garlic, and blend until smooth. Add salt and cayenne pepper, and blend. Garnish with parsley, and serve.

Nutritional Information per Serving
Calories 28, Protein (g) 1, Carbohydrate (g) 3, Fat (g) 2, Calories from Fat (%) 54, Saturated Fat (g) 0, Dietary Fiber (g) 1, Cholesterol (mg) 0, Sodium (mg) 2
Diabetic Exchanges: *0.5 fat*

Terrific Tip
TAHINI IS A THICK PASTE MADE FROM GROUND SESAME SEEDS AND USED AS A FLAVORING IN MIDDLE EASTERN COOKING. LOOK FOR IT SOLD IN CANS IN THE MIDDLE EASTERN OR ASIAN SECTION AT MOST SUPERMARKETS.

LAYERED SUN-DRIED TOMATO, PINE NUT, AND SPINACH SPREAD

Layered Sun-dried Tomato, Pine Nut, and Spinach Spread

This eye-catching, make-ahead, layered spread is packed with great ingredients and tons of flavor. Serve with crackers or toast points.

MAKES 15 TO 20 SERVINGS

2 (8-ounce) packages reduced-fat cream cheese, softened

1 (8-ounce) package feta cheese, drained of liquid

1 teaspoon minced garlic

1 teaspoon hot sauce

Salt and pepper, to taste

2/3 cup chopped sun-dried tomatoes (not oil-packed)

1/4 cup pine nuts, toasted (see Terrific Tip, page 22)

1/2 cup finely chopped fresh parsley

1/2 cup sliced green onions (scallions)

1 cup finely chopped fresh baby spinach

Line an 8½ x 4½ x 2½-inch loaf pan with plastic wrap, and coat the plastic with nonstick cooking spray.

In a mixer, beat together the cream cheese, feta, garlic, hot sauce, salt, and pepper until creamy, and set aside. Pour 1 cup of boiling water over the sun-dried tomatoes, and let sit for 10 minutes to soften.

Cover the bottom of the loaf pan with the pine nuts. Layer the parsley over the pine nuts, and then layer the green onions. Carefully spread with one-third of the cream cheese mixture to cover the green onions, keeping the layers intact. Drain the water from the sun-dried tomatoes, and spread the tomatoes over the cream cheese layer. Next, carefully spread one-third of the cream cheese mixture over the tomatoes, being careful not to mix. Evenly cover the cream cheese with the chopped spinach. Carefully spread the remaining one-third of the cream cheese on top to cover the spinach, being careful not to mix. Cover, and refrigerate until ready to serve. To serve, place the pan upside down on a serving plate, lift off the pan, and carefully remove the plastic wrap.

Nutritional Information per Serving

Calories 102, Protein (g) 5, Carbohydrate (g) 3, Fat (g) 8, Calories from Fat (%) 71, Saturated Fat (g) 5, Dietary Fiber (g) 0, Cholesterol (mg) 26, Sodium (mg) 228
Diabetic Exchanges: *1 lean meat, 1 fat*

Marinated Shrimp

Serve this marvelous recipe in a glass bowl with frilled toothpicks to highlight the wonderful seafood selection.

MAKES 10 SERVINGS

1/4 cup ketchup

2 tablespoons prepared horseradish

2 tablespoons lemon juice

2 tablespoons grainy mustard

1 tablespoon olive oil

1 teaspoon hot pepper sauce

1 teaspoon minced garlic

1/3 cup sliced green onions (scallions)

2 tablespoons capers, drained

2 pounds peeled medium or
large shrimp, cooked

In a medium bowl, mix together the ketchup, horseradish, lemon juice, mustard, olive oil, hot sauce, and garlic. Add the green onions and capers. Add the shrimp, stirring to coat well with the ketchup mixture. Cover and refrigerate until chilled, at least 1 to 2 hours, before serving.

Nutritional Information per Serving
Calories 115, Protein (g) 19, Carbohydrate (g) 3, Fat (g) 2, Calories from Fat (%) 20, Saturated Fat (g) 0, Dietary Fiber (g) 0, Cholesterol (mg) 177, Sodium (mg) 411
Diabetic Exchanges: *3 very lean meat*

Smoked Salmon and Caviar Dip

Impress your guests with salmon and caviar united in a no-fuss dip with lots of class. Serve with toast points.

MAKES 24 (2-TABLESPOON) SERVINGS

2 (8-ounce) packages reduced-fat
cream cheese, softened

3 tablespoons nonfat sour cream

1/2 teaspoon dried dill weed leaves

4 ounces thinly sliced smoked salmon,
cut into small pieces

1/2 cup chopped green onion (scallion)
stems

Pepper, to taste

1 (2-ounce) jar red salmon caviar

Minced chives, for garnish

In a mixing bowl, beat the cream cheese for 2 minutes, until light and creamy. Beat in the sour cream and dill. Stir in the salmon and green onion stems. Season with pepper. Gently fold in the caviar. Cover, and refrigerate for at least 1 hour. Sprinkle with chives before servings.

Nutritional Information per Serving
Calories 62, Protein (g) 4, Carbohydrate (g) 1, Fat (g) 5, Calories from Fat (%) 70, Saturated Fat (g) 3, Dietary Fiber (g) 0, Cholesterol (mg) 29, Sodium (mg) 213
Diabetic Exchanges: *0.5 very lean meat, 1 fat*

Terrific Tip

TO LOWER THE FAT CONTENT OF THIS RECIPE, YOU MAY SUBSTITUTE FAT-FREE CREAM CHEESE FOR ONE OR BOTH OF THE PACKAGES OF REDUCED-FAT CREAM CHEESE.

Terrific Tip

AN OVERFLOWING BOWL OF DIFFERENT COLORED GRAPES CAN BE AS IMPRESSIVE AS A FLOWER ARRANGEMENT. USE FRUIT AS ACCENTS TO ENTERTAINING DISHWARE.

Layered Crabmeat, Guacamole, and Tomato Dip

The combination of colors, flavors, and textures makes you cherish every bite of this layered extravaganza. The touch of cumin adds a nice, Southwestern flavor. If crabmeat is not available, substitute small shrimp. Serve with sturdy chips or crackers.

MAKES 8 TO 10 SERVINGS

2 cups chopped tomatoes (yellow and red)
1 tablespoon olive oil
Salt and pepper, to taste
1/4 cup light mayonnaise
2 tablespoons nonfat sour cream
1/4 cup chopped red onion
1 tablespoon lime juice
1/2 teaspoon minced garlic
1/4 teaspoon ground cumin
1 pound lump crabmeat, picked for shells
Guacamole (recipe follows)

GUACAMOLE:
1 cup coarsely chopped avocados
2 tablespoons finely chopped red onion
1 tablespoon lime juice
1 tablespoon nonfat sour cream
1 tablespoon chopped jalapeño peppers
1/2 teaspoon ground cumin
1/8 teaspoon cayenne pepper
Salt and pepper, to taste

In a bowl, toss the tomatoes with the olive oil, salt, and pepper, and refrigerate until ready to assemble. In a bowl, mix together the mayonnaise, sour cream, red onion, lime juice, garlic, and cumin. Fold in the crabmeat, and refrigerate until ready to assemble.

When ready to assemble, spread a layer of Guacamole over a platter. Drain the tomatoes, and layer over the Guacamole. Carefully spoon the crabmeat mixture on top.

Guacamole; In a bowl, mix together the avocados, onion, lime juice, sour cream, jalapeño peppers, cumin, cayenne, salt, and pepper, mashing slightly to combine. Refrigerate until ready to serve.

Nutritional Information per Serving
Calories 124, Protein (g) 11, Carbohydrate (g) 6, Fat (g) 6,
Calories from Fat (%) 46, Saturated Fat (g) 1, Dietary Fiber (g) 1,
Cholesterol (mg) 37, Sodium (mg) 227
Diabetic Exchanges: *1.5 lean meat, 1 vegetable*

Terrific Tip
TO MAKE CRAB CAKES AHEAD OF TIME, REFRIGERATE THE COOKED CRAB CAKES UNTIL READY TO SERVE. REHEAT THEM IN A SINGLE LAYER IN A PREHEATED 350°F OVEN FOR 10 MINUTES, OR UNTIL THOROUGHLY HEATED.

Miniature Crab Cakes with Horseradish Sauce

Preparing the crab cakes ahead of time makes this gourmet wonder easy and organized.

MAKES 24 MINIATURE CRAB CAKES

1/2 cup sliced green onions (scallions)
2 tablespoons finely chopped onion
1 large egg, slightly beaten
1/3 cup light mayonnaise
1 tablespoon Dijon mustard
1 teaspoon lime juice
1/2 teaspoon dried thyme leaves
Dash crushed red pepper flakes
1 pint lump crabmeat, picked for shells
4 cups corn flakes
2 tablespoons chopped fresh parsley
Horseradish Sauce (recipe follows)

HORSERADISH SAUCE:
2/3 cup light mayonnaise
1 1/2 tablespoons prepared horseradish
1 1/2 tablespoons Dijon mustard

In a bowl, mix together the green onions, onion, egg, mayonnaise, mustard, lime juice, thyme, and red pepper flakes. Carefully stir in the crabmeat until mixed. Shape the crabmeat mixture into 2-inch miniature crab cakes. In a food processor, process the corn flakes into fine crumbs, and mix with the parsley. Spread the crumb mixture on a large plate. Coat each crab cake with the cornflake mixture and lay on a baking sheet lined with wax paper. Refrigerate until ready to cook.

To serve, coat a nonstick skillet with nonstick cooking spray, and set over medium-high heat. Cook the crab cakes, turning once, until golden brown on both sides, about 10 minutes. Serve with Horseradish Sauce for dipping.

Horseradish Sauce: In a small bowl, combine the mayonnaise, horseradish, and mustard, mixing well. Refrigerate.

Nutritional Information per Serving (per crab cake)
Calories 67, Protein (g) 3, Carbohydrate (g) 5, Fat (g) 4, Calories from Fat (%) 52,
Saturated Fat (g) 1, Dietary Fiber (g) 0, Cholesterol (mg) 22, Sodium (mg) 182
Diabetic Exchanges: *0.5 starch, 1 fat*

SHRIMP CHIPOLTE CUPS

Shrimp Chipotle Cups

These creative and enticing cups are simple to make with won ton wrappers, a jar of roasted red peppers, and cooked shrimp. They're eye appealing and addicting, so be sure to make plenty! Won ton wrappers are usually sold in the refrigerated produce section of the supermarket, alongside other Asian ingredients like fresh noodles and tofu.

MAKES 36 CUPS

3 dozen won ton wrappers

1½ cups shredded reduced-fat
Monterey Jack cheese

1 cup cooked, peeled, and coarsely
chopped shrimp

1 cup chopped roasted red peppers, drained

1 cup chipotle salsa
(see Terrific Tip, page 48)

½ cup sliced green onions (scallions)

Preheat the oven to 350°F. Coat a mini muffin pan with nonstick cooking spray, and press a won ton wrapper into each cup. Bake 7 to 9 minutes, or until golden brown.

Meanwhile, in a bowl, combine the cheese, shrimp, roasted red peppers, salsa, and green onions. Remove the cooked won tons, fill each with some of the shrimp mixture, and continue baking 8 to 10 minutes, or until the cheese is melted.

Nutritional Information per Serving (per cup)
Calories 47, Protein (g) 3, Carbohydrate (g) 5, Fat (g) 2,
Calories from Fat (%) 32, Saturated Fat (g) 1,
Dietary Fiber (g) 0, Cholesterol (mg) 11, Sodium (mg) 75
Diabetic Exchanges: *0.5 lean meat, 0.5 starch*

Terrific Tip
YOU CAN SUBSTITUTE PRE-COOKED CHICKEN FOR THE SHRIMP IN THIS RECIPE—LEFTOVER GRILLED CHICKEN MAKES A CONVENIENT AND TASTY VARIATION.

Pepper Dijon Tenderloin

This is an exceptional beef recipe and a guaranteed hit of the party. Marinate ahead of time, and pop into the oven when ready to cook. I really couldn't decide for which party this recipe was best suited; it also makes a fabulous dinner entrée for any special meal. Tenderloin is an expensive cut of meat but worth every bite.

MAKES 20 TO 24 SERVINGS

1 (5- to 6-pound) whole tenderloin,
  trimmed of excess fat
Salt and pepper, to taste
1/2 cup fat-free Italian dressing
1/2 cup Worcestershire sauce
1/2 cup Dijon mustard
Coarsely cracked black pepper

Lay the tenderloin in a glass dish, and season with salt and pepper. Cover and pat the tenderloin with the Italian dressing and Worcestershire sauce. Cover with plastic wrap, and refrigerate for 48 hours, time permitting. Let the meat come to room temperature before cooking (for at least 1 hour).

Preheat the oven to 500°F. Pour off and discard the marinade, cover the meat with the Dijon mustard, and season heavily with cracked black pepper. Transfer to a baking dish. Cook for 12 minutes, then reduce the oven temperature to 275°F, and cook for another 25 to 30 minutes, depending on the desired doneness.

Nutritional Information per Serving
Calories 180, Protein (g) 24, Carbohydrate (g) 0, Fat (g) 8, Calories from Fat (%) 43,
Saturated Fat (g) 3, Dietary Fiber (g) 0, Cholesterol (mg) 71, Sodium (mg) 350
Diabetic Exchanges: *3 lean meat*

Goat Cheese and Green Onion Scones

The green onions and goat cheese give these scones a wonderfully different taste that makes them a treat by themselves, though they are the perfect accompaniment to the Pepper Dijon Tenderloin (previous recipe). They are absolutely delicious when served warm, right from the oven.

MAKES 24 SCONES

4 cup all-purpose flour
2 tablespoons baking powder
Salt and pepper, to taste
6 ounces herb and garlic goat cheese, crumbled
1/2 cup sliced green onions (scallions)
1 1/2 cups fat-free half & half
2 eggs

Preheat the oven to 375°F. Coat a baking sheet with nonstick cooking spray.

In a bowl, combine the flour, baking powder, salt, and pepper, and mix well. Add the cheese and green onions, stirring with a fork to combine. In a small bowl, mix together the half & half and eggs until slightly beaten. Add to the flour mixture, stirring until the mixture forms a ball. Roll out the dough on waxed paper on a floured surface to about ¾-inch thick. Cut with a biscuit cutter or a 2-inch glass to make rounds. Place on the prepared baking sheet, and bake for 20 to 25 minutes, or until lightly browned.

Nutritional Information per Serving (per scone)
Calories 115, Protein (g) 5, Carbohydrate (g) 19, Fat (g) 2, Calories from Fat (%) 17,
Saturated Fat (g) 1, Dietary Fiber (g) 1, Cholesterol (mg) 23, Sodium (mg) 199
Diabetic Exchanges: *1.5 starch*

Terrific Tip
WHO HAS TIME TO SHINE SILVER THESE DAYS? I NOW ENTERTAIN USING PEWTER PIECES, SOME OF WHICH CAN EVEN GO IN THE OVEN.

Sesame Chicken Bites with Sweet and Spicy Sauce

A touch of Asian influence makes this an especially good "pop in your mouth" chicken recipe.

MAKES 16 TO 20 SERVINGS

3/4 cup honey

3/4 cup reduced-sodium soy sauce

1 tablespoon sesame oil

1 teaspoon minced garlic

1/2 teaspoon crushed red pepper flakes

1/3 cup sesame seeds, toasted
(see Terrific Tip, page 00)

2 pounds boneless, skinless chicken breasts,
cut into 2-inch cubes

Sweet and Spicy Sauce (recipe follows),
for dipping

In a 2-quart glass dish, mix together the honey, soy sauce, sesame oil, garlic, and red pepper flakes. Add the chicken, and stir to cover. Marinate for at least 1 hour or overnight.

Preheat the oven to 375°F. Coat a baking sheet with nonstick cooking spray.

Spread the sesame seeds on a plate, and roll the chicken in the seeds to cover. Place the chicken on the prepared baking sheet. Bake for 20 minutes, or until the chicken is done.

Serve with the Sweet and Spicy Sauce, for dipping.

***Nutritional Information per Serving
(without the Sweet and Spicy Sauce)***
Calories 74, Protein (g) 12, Carbohydrate (g) 1, Fat (g) 2, Calories from Fat (%) 25,
Saturated Fat (g) 0, Dietary Fiber (g) 0, Cholesterol (mg) 26, Sodium (mg) 267
Diabetic Exchanges: *2 very lean meat*

Sweet and Spicy Sauce

Just three simple ingredients combine to create this incredible sauce.

MAKES 20 SERVINGS

1 cup orange marmalade

1 tablespoon prepared horseradish sauce

2 tablespoons Dijon mustard

In a small bowl, mix together the orange marmalade, horseradish sauce, and mustard. Refrigerate until ready to use.

Nutritional Information per 20 Servings
Calories 41, Protein (g) 0, Carbohydrate (g) 11, Fat (g) 0, Calories from Fat (%) 0,
Saturated Fat (g) 0, Dietary Fiber (g) 0, Cholesterol (mg) 0, Sodium (mg) 47
Diabetic Exchanges: *0.5 other carbohydrate*

Terrific Tips

HORS D'OEUVRES SERVING SIZES:

▶ 8 TO 10 PIECES PER PERSON FOR LIGHT
HORS D'OEUVRES.

▶ 15 PIECES PER PERSON FOR PRIME-TIME,
HEAVY HORS D'OEUVRES.

▶ EXPECT EACH GUEST TO USE ABOUT 3
NAPKINS AND 3 PLASTIC GLASSES.

▶ ALLOT 1 POUND OF ICE PER PERSON. ICE IS
CHEAP, AND IT'S VERY FRUSTRATING IF YOU
RUN OUT OF IT, SO STOCK UP!

GLAZED APRICOT ALMOND BRIE

Glazed Apricot Almond Brie

Every time I throw a party, I always include baked Brie, and every time, the Brie steals the show. This impressive Brie recipe will win over everyone. I've included directions to serve the Brie warm from the oven; however, the apricot preserves may be heated in the microwave and the Brie may be served at room temperature. It's best served with assorted crackers and apple slices.

MAKES 20 SERVINGS

14 ounces Brie
1/2 cup apricot preserves
1 tablespoon orange liqueur or orange juice
1/4 cup sliced almonds, toasted
(see Terrific Tip, page 22)

Preheat the oven to 325°F.

Remove the top rind of the Brie. Place the Brie in a shallow baking dish. Mix together the apricot preserves and orange liqueur, and spread on top of the Brie. Bake for 8 to 10 minutes, or just until the Brie is soft and heated through. Remove from the oven, and sprinkle with the almonds. Serve immediately.

Terrific Tip

IF YOU ARE USING CHINA PLATES, DON'T WORRY ABOUT HAVING ENOUGH OF ONE PATTERN. I THINK IT'S FUN TO USE ALL OF YOUR PATTERNS MIXED TOGETHER.

Nutritional Information per Serving
Calories 95, Protein (g) 4, Carbohydrate (g) 6, Fat (g) 6, Calories from Fat (%) 57, Saturated Fat (g) 4, Dietary Fiber (g) 0, Cholesterol (mg) 20, Sodium (mg) 128
Diabetic Exchanges: *0.5 lean meat, 0.5 other carbohydrate, 1 fat*

Terrific Tip

FOR ANOTHER BRIE SENSATION, MIX TOGETHER ¼ CUP BROWN SUGAR AND ¼-CUP COFFEE LIQUEUR UNTIL THE SUGAR DISSOLVES. TOP THE BRIE WITH THIS MIXTURE, BAKE AS INSTRUCTED IN THE MAIN RECIPE, AND TOP WITH TOASTED PECANS. SOMETIMES I SERVE TWO BRIES WITH TWO DIFFERENT TOPPINGS, SIDE BY SIDE

Terrific Tip

AN APPLE SWAN MAKES A BEAUTIFUL, ARTISTIC GARNISH. YOU NEED TWO APPLES, ONE FOR THE BODY AND ONE FOR THE HEAD. CUT OFF A THIN SLICE FROM THE BOTTOM OF ONE APPLE TO PROVIDE A FLAT BASE. ON ONE SIDE, USE A SERRATED KNIFE IN A LIGHT SAWING MOTION TO MAKE A SMALL WEDGE CUT AT THE TOP. CONTINUE MAKING WEDGE SHAPED CUTS, EACH A BIT LARGER THAN THE PREVIOUS ONE. REPEAT THIS ON THE OTHER SIDES, FORMING THREE SETS OF WINGS. IF A PIECE BREAKS, THE SECTIONS WILL FIT TOGETHER AND THE BREAK WILL NOT BE NOTICEABLE. STARTING WITH THE LARGEST CUT, OVERLAP CONSECUTIVE SMALLER CUTS, FANNING OUT THE WINGS. STICK A TOOTHPICK DEEP IN TO HOLD WINGS IN PLACE. TO FORM THE HEAD AND NECK, CUT A ½-INCH SLICE FROM THE WEDGE OF THE OTHER APPLE. CARVE A NECK AND USE A CLOVE FOR THE EYE. CUT A SMALL WEDGE IN THE FRONT OF THE APPLE, AND ATTACH THE HEAD AND NECK WITH TOOTHPICK. PREVENT DARKENING BY SQUEEZING LEMON JUICE OVER THE ENTIRE SURFACE OF THE BIRD (OR YOU CAN PURCHASE A COMMERCIAL PRODUCT FROM THE GROCERY STORE, SOLD FOR THE SPECIFIC PURPOSE OF PREVENTING THE DARKENING OF FRUIT).

Index